Dorset Shipwrecks

Frontispiece
The rescue harness being used to bring ashore some of the passengers from the emigrant vessel Royal Adelaide *in November 1872.*

Dorset Shipwrecks

David Burnett

THE DOVECOTE PRESS

First published in 1982 by The Dovecote Press
Stanbridge, Wimborne, Dorset
ISBN 0 946159 04 1

Designed by Humphrey Stone

Photoset in English Times
Printed and bound in Great Britain

Contents

Introduction

The Dorset coast has not been kind to ships, nor to those who sail them. The recovery of a stone anchor from the sea off Lulworth Cove, and the discovery of Roman coins off the Chesil, suggest that Roman galleys may be amongst its earliest victims. In the waters off Portland and the Chesil Beach it boasts perhaps the most crowded graveyard in the Channel. There can be few headlands, shoals and ledges along the rest of its length that do not mark where a ship once struck.

Waves breaking over the schooner Madelaine Tristan *after it had struck in Chesil Cove on September 20th 1930 when bound in ballast for Le Havre.*

Despite its attractions to those who live ashore, sailors have always found it to be bleak and unforgiving. Tides and races make navigation difficult. Portland's stone fist divides the exposed waters of Lyme Bay from the cliffs of Purbeck. There are few places where sailing ships could run for shelter, and only a handful of anchorages: Poole, Studland and Swanage Bays, Lulworth Cove, Weymouth, Portland Roads, Bridport Harbour, the haven offered by the Cobb at Lyme Regis. Of these, two are man made, and only Poole and Weymouth are secure in all weathers.

Shipwrecks are not the romantic events that some imagine them to be. There is little

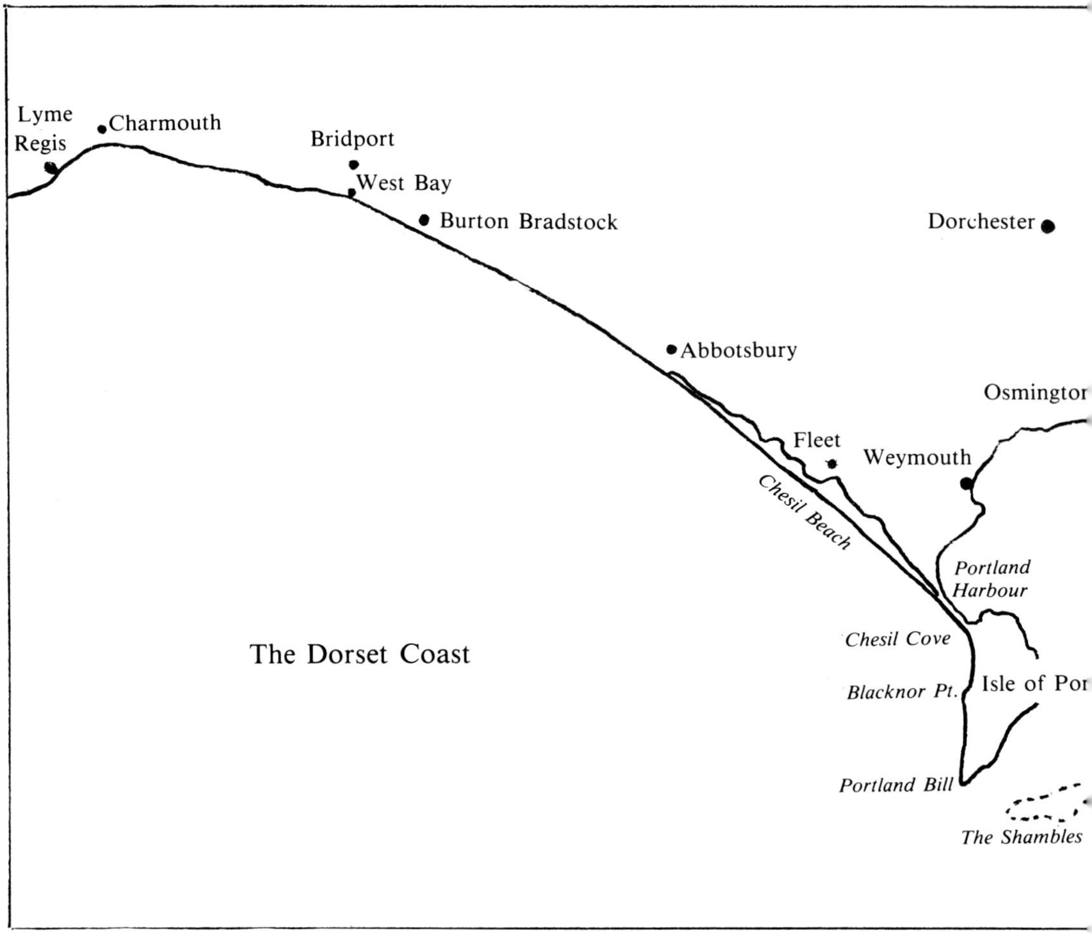

of the comic about them; each has its own tales of grief, error, heroism and suffering. Ships have foundered in all weathers and in all seasons. There is evidence that as early as the middle ages a house for sheltering shipwrecked sailors stood behind the Chesil. On Christmas Day 1600 more than twenty ships were wrecked off the Chesil, including the privateer *Isobel* and the Spanish vessel it had been pursuing up Channel. In one tragic night in 1795 six ships struck on the Beach and 298 people are known to have drowned. The events of November 1824 have entered legend as the 'Great Gale'. Many wrecks have gone unrecorded, victims of carelessness or the south-westerly gales that can suddenly sweep the Channel, their sole memorial a few shattered timbers or a drowned body washed up on the beach, perhaps months later. Some retain an air of mystery, as when a wreck was found ashore at Osmington in 1742, 'sunk, not any living sole belonging to her, nor any papers to describe to whom she belonged.'

The recovery of casks of wine from that same vessel tells us much about the nature of many wrecks. For the Channel is a commercial artery, and in the days of the sailing ship it served the merchant in Amsterdam or Bordeaux as well as the inshore coastal trade. Shipping outward bound from Portsmouth or Southampton traditionally crossed Poole Bay. A French fishing smack blown off course could easily break its back on Portland. Poole's first lifeboat first put to sea in 1867 to take off the crew of a German

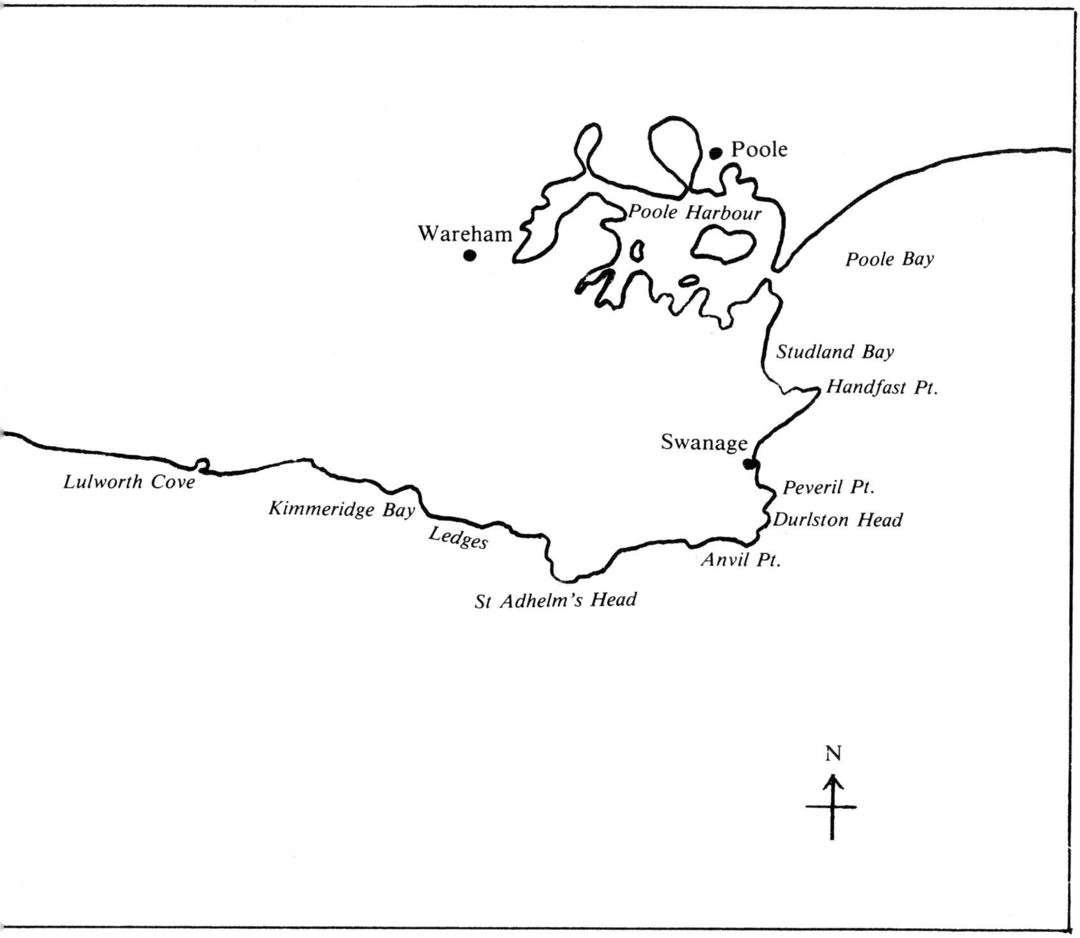

brig that had foundered on the Hook Sands with a cargo of Portuguese cork. Emigrant ships, revenue cutters, East Indiamen, the casualties of war – all lie at rest in the waters off Dorset. A few have left a permanent legacy. Since the Greek steamer *Elena R* sank after hitting a mine off the Shambles in 1939, the tidal streams caused by the wreck have created a ridge of broken shells that stretches for half-a-mile.

Nor did a ship's size or condition confer immunity from disaster. The steamer *Treveal* was returning from Calcutta after its maiden voyage, when it grounded on the Kimmeridge Ledges in 1920. When the 1,250 ton *Alexandrovna* was driven ashore near Tilly Whim in 1882 its entire seventy-seven man crew was drowned; the ship itself broke up in less than ten minutes and it was only the discovery of an empty ship's boat that enabled it to be identified.

But much of the shipping wrecked along the Dorset coast was launched in local yards and crewed by Dorset men; ships like the tiny 60 ton cogs that rounded Old Harry every spring on the voyage to the Newfoundland fisheries, the luggers and schooners that once plied from port to port with the goods that had brought the county its wealth – Bridport netting, stone from Portland and Purbeck. Cargoes such as these did little to lessen the chances of tragedy. No Dorset port is as hazardous to enter as West Bay; the crews that worked the stone ships risked death on every voyage.

It was the fate of vessels such as these that

A painting showing the scene on the Chesil after the 2,000 ton emigrant clipper Royal Adelaide *had grounded opposite Ferry Bridge during a south-westerly gale on the night of November 25th 1872.*

brought home the realities of shipwreck, creating a folk-lore that still endures. The ghostly pealing of bells is supposed to be audible off Handfast Point during a gale, a reminder of a ship carrying bells for a Poole church that went down off the Point because of the blasphemy of its crew. Following the loss of the *Royal Adelaide* on the Chesil in 1872 'the naked body of a most beautiful woman' was washed up on the Beach. Looters were preparing to sever her fingers to remove the rings when a stranger, passing in his coach, carried her away with the intention of burying her. Her sudden revival and their eventual marriage only improves the myth.

As well as being a rich source of legend, wrecks have brought more profitable spoils. Throughout the middle ages they became crown property once ashore and abandoned (even the presence of a dog left on board was sufficient to maintain their original ownership). In Dorset, the crown granted most of its Rights of Wreck to others, usually the monastic houses or feudal nobility. Milton Abbey held the Rights at Osmington and in the mouth of the River Frome. The Abbey of Cerne acquired Kimmeridge and Bridport Creek, whilst the Earls of Gloucester owned all wrecks at Weymouth, Wyke, and on Portland.

By the 17th century it was no longer the Church who profited, but those who lived by the sea. At times their behaviour was far from perfect. References to the 'law-less barn-door savages of the coast,' to a beach 'lined with men, women and children whose only object was plunder,' are all too commonplace. When the Dutch merchantman *Hope* broke up on the Chesil in 1749 carrying bullion worth £50,000 organized gangs looted its remains. Attempts by customs men

A drawing of a Portland lerret by William Pye, circa *1895. The lerret's wide beam and flat bottom made it the ideal boat for the Chesil. Most were about 20 feet long, rowed double-banked with six oars, and they were traditionally both launched and landed with their bows facing the sea.*

to recover the cargo from a ship wrecked on Portland in 1716, led to them being 'Beat, Hounded and Resisted . . . in the Salvidge' by looters.

Yet it is easy to exaggerate such incidents. Against them must be balanced the unsung bravery of those who chanced their lives to save others; the men of the Coastguard and Lifeboat Services, the fishermen of Portland and Wyke Regis putting to sea in their small six-oared lerrets in order to take off the crews and passengers of vessels on the brink of foundering. Even dogs have played their part, as when a dog, bred on Portland, swam out with a line after the *Thomas & Mary* had sunk off Sandsfoot Castle in 1879.

The acts of heroism are important. For although the sea is always the villain, there are times when it may seem that it is not people who are the true heroes of this book, but the ships themselves. Perhaps that is inevitable? To those who sail them, ships acquire a character that is uniquely their own. What unites those mentioned in the pages that follow is that all were doomed, and ended their days as victims of the seas off Dorset.

Poole Harbour to St Alban's Head

The first known nautical disaster to have occurred near Poole remains the worst in Dorset's history: more ships were wrecked, more lives were undoubtedly lost than at any time since. Perhaps inevitably, its background was conflict: its participants were Saxon and Viking.

In 877, Alfred was king of Wessex and Wareham was a Viking stronghold. That spring, the Vikings left the town by sea with the intention of raising Alfred's blockade of Exeter. Some sixty-oared Saxon galleys, built to their monarch's design, trailed the Viking Fleet as it crossed Poole Harbour and broke out into Studland Bay. Off Peveril Point, the wind increased and veered to the east. The Viking longships with their low freeboard were soon shipping water. They were caught on a lee shore, with anchors that would not grip on the loose sandy bottom. Heavy seas, a gale force wind and the notorious race off Peveril Point now combined to bring their voyage to a premature end. By the time the wind had dropped, more than a hundred longships had foundered or been swept on to the rocks.

The sinking of another hostile ship, the *San Salvador*, in those same waters more than 700 years later in November 1588 raises issues posed all too frequently by this book – human error and human fallibility. The 958 ton *San Salvador* had sailed with the ill-fated Spanish Armada as the flagship of the Paymaster General. After catching fire and being severely damaged off Portland, the Portuguese built carrack had been boarded by a prize crew and brought into Portland Roads, 'much splitted and torn' and with men manning the pumps to prevent her sinking. It was an opportunity Weymouth's cannon-starved mayor wasted no time in exploiting, and he immediately requested the use of the carrack's ordnance to defend the town. At first the Council agreed to his request, with the provision that some of the twenty-five cannons be given to Lyme Regis, and Corfe and Portland Castles. The Council then revoked its decision, demanding that all the *San Salvador*'s ordnance be sent to London. By then the ship had been stripped of anything of value. A treasure chest is now in Weymouth Museum. Much of the powder had vanished, and the local justices were complaining about the cost of mounting a guard on the prize to prevent further looting. In October it was decided that the *San Salvador* should be moved to Portsmouth Dockyard. A muddle over a new sail promised, but not delivered, by the captain of Portland Castle led to the ship sailing inadequately rigged and badly lightened by the removal of its cannons. In Studland Bay it capsized and sank, causing the deaths of twenty-three men.

Such episodes owe more to carelessness and poor seamanship than they do to wind and weather. But the hazards confronting a helmsman entering any of Dorset's harbours should not be underestimated. Poole provides a perfect example. Few serious mishaps ever took place in the Harbour (though those that did claimed many lives), but Poole's importance as a port and the good fortune that gives it a second high water kept the channel between North and South Haven Points constantly busy. With the wind in the west Studland Bay is a good holding ground, but the proximity of the Milkmaid Shoal and the Hook Sands caused many ships to run aground when making for Swash Channel.

Shipping at Poole Quay in 1891. The volume of shipping using the port helps explain the number of wrecks that took place either side of the approach Channel into the Harbour.

Wrecks ring the Harbour entrance, some of them victims of the ugly seas that can break over the bar when the tide is ebbing and the wind in the south-east.

The list of such ships is endless. The two *Fame*'s: one bound for Newfoundland in 1788 when it grounded and the strain on the hull opened up the caulking and planking; the other a steam-drifter that grounded on the Hook Sands in 1916 and whose seven-man crew had to be taken off by Poole lifeboat, the *Harmar*. The *Bee*, a West Indiaman outward bound from London in 1799, that had struck after taking shelter during a gale and whose crew was rescued by Charles Sturt, M.P. for Bridport and owner of Brownsea Island, and taken to his 'hospitable mansion': Sturt's charity was rewarded, the following year he capsized in his yacht off Portland and would certainly have drowned had he not been sighted and picked up by a military transport.

There are a succession of memorable rescues associated with the approaches to Poole. In 1852, the *William Glen Anderson*, a Poole barque, was returning from Quebec when it was driven ashore near Boscombe and its crew had to be taken off by a Lieutenant Parsons of the Bournebottom Coastguard Station and four of his men – a rescue that won Parsons the Insitution's silver medal. Fourteen years later two French luggers, the *Jeune Erneste* and the *Augustine*, simultaneously grounded in heavy seas either side of the channel after mistaking Poole for Portsmouth – an error that seems almost implausible. The survival of the crews was due entirely to the anonymous lady who three years earlier in 1865 had given Poole its first lifeboat, the 32 feet ten-oared *Manley Wood*. The lifeboat was soon launched from its house on Sandbanks, and after taking off the four men on the *Jeune Erneste* it helped refloat the *Augustine* and nurse it into safer waters. Others have been equally fortunate. In 1910 the engines failed on the 4,000 ton *Leander* off Durlston Head. The steamer finally drifted ashore at Canford Cliffs, with its bows almost touching the cliff. Four months later it was refloated, but so fast had it stuck that for much of the time the captain and his family were able to take up residence on board. Another ship to be refloated after striking was the Norwegian three-masted schooner *Frier*. After the schooner's crew had been taken off by lifeboat in heavy seas in November 1898, it finally grounded at Flag Head Chine, from where it was later salvaged, repaired and refitted for sea. But the *Frier* was doomed. In November 1903, in passage from Antwerp to Newcastle, it was blown off course in a North Sea gale and wrecked on Terschelling Sands.

For most ships, the calmer waters of Poole Harbour meant refuge from the storm. An entire alphabet of vessels, ranging from the brig *Antares* to the motor-schooner *Zwaluw*, would have been safe had they rounded North Haven Point, until the turn of the century the deserted sand-bank that has since provided it with a new name. Some however, ended their days in the shallows of the Harbour, and the two most tragic disasters to take place in the Harbour both involved passenger boats who daily plied its waters. The first happened in March 1759 when the Poole to Ower passage boat was stranded in mud, and thirteen out of the nineteen people on board were drowned trying to reach Furzey Island. Only the superstitious will derive meaning from the numbers, for it can surely be no more than chance that the second disaster also involved a passage boat and ended in thirteen deaths? At dusk, on October 2nd 1806, the Wareham to Poole

Swanage's fourth lifeboat, the 40 feet Thomas Markby, *shortly before its official launching in July 1928. The* Thomas Markby *had a 40 h.p. engine, and it saved 27 lives during its 21 years of service.*

ferry ran aground off Swineham Point as it entered the Frome. It was foggy, and raining. As well as the owner and two boatmen, there were twelve passengers on board. The boat must have then capsized, for we know that the current filled the sails, forcing it under the water and making it difficult for those on board to reach the surface and swim clear. There were two survivors; Mr Everett of Wareham, who swam ashore and raised the alarm after guiding Mrs White to an oar and making certain she was safe.

Happily, such tragedies have been few in the Harbour, but once outside the entrance and at the mercy of the open sea their numbers swiftly increase. Even Old Harry Rock has claimed his victims, as did his Wife before she fell in 1896. Eddies wash round both Ballard and Handfast Points, and a race can build up round the latter during a west-flowing tide. There is another race off Durlston Head; and another off Peveril Point, where the tide sets strongly off the ledges, and cross-currents and rogue winds can create a vicious steeply sloped swell.

One casualty of Old Harry was the naval trawler *King Heron*, on war-time patrol in 1915 when it struck the ledge. The crew of ten was safely taken off by lifeboat before the trawler went down, but other war-time wrecks along this section of the coast have ended more tragically. The *Kyarra* began life as a Clyde-built steamer sailing in Australian waters. With the outbreak of war in 1914 it was converted into a hospital ship, first taking off the wounded during the Dardanelles campaign and then serving in the Channel. In May 1918 the 4,500 ton steamer was empty of passengers and outward bound for Sydney with a general cargo when it was torpedoed off Durlston Head. It sank immediately in a hundred feet of water and six of its crew were drowned. It remains there today, almost intact, its' holds still laden with perfume, textiles and wine – a breathtaking sight to the divers who visit it.

As well as marking the final resting-place of many war-time losses, the seas off Dorset conceal their share of foreign shipping. The prevailing Channel wind is a westerly, and even a slight movement to the south can lead to French coastal shipping being blown badly off course. The hazards of so rocky a lee-shore merely have to assist with the *coup de grâce*. In 1838, the *Aimable Mere, en route* from Dunkirk to Bordeaux, foundered off St Alban's Head and the crew of seven were rescued by the coastguard. In 1865 the lugger *Virginie* struck the same headland and was soon destroyed. Nor have other nations been any more fortunate. In January 1879, the *Anne Margretha*, a 500 ton Norwegian barque bound in ballast for Baltimore from Rouen, was driven on to Ballard Point in seas so heavy, its' remains fetched only £45 at auction. The master, his daughter and the crew of ten were all saved, but the loss of the *Anne Margretha* was further proof of the need for a lighthouse in the area. The site chosen was Anvil Point, where a Telegraph & Signal Station already stood, and by the end of 1881 the house had been built and its light was in operation.

For some ships the opening of the lighthouse on Anvil Point made little difference to their fate. It was only four months later, in the spring of 1882, that the *Alexandrovna* was driven ashore in a south-south-westerly gale on to the rocks west of the lighthouse. Wrecks such as these can lose their meaning if too many are listed. But one shipwreck associated with Purbeck cannot be ignored. Some wrecks acquire a significance that verges on the legendary, and the destruction of the *Halsewell* on Seacombe Cliffs in 1786 is just such a wreck.

It was on New Year's Day that the 785 ton East Indiaman set sail from Gravesend for Madras with 242 people on board. For Captain Pierce, the oldest officer in the Service, it was to be his final voyage before retirement, and amongst the seven female passengers were his two daughters and two of his nieces. Their presence does no credit to their parents, for all seven were being deliberately despatched to India in hope of attracting husbands. The voyage began badly. Snow and bitter winds accompanied the *Halsewell* down Channel, making the sails so heavy with ice that the mizen-mast

Survivors from the Halsewell *at the base of Seacombe Cliffs after the East Indiaman had begun breaking up in February 1786.*

had to be cut away. The weather worsened, a westerly gale adding to the amount of water being shipped through the hawse-holes in the bows. A leak was then discovered, and with nearly seven feet of water in the bilges the *Halsewell* took longer to straighten between rolls. At this juncture, sections of the crew refused to work the pumps and instead 'skulked in their hammocks.' To prevent the ship foundering it was decided to fell the main-mast with axes, but the coxswain and four seamen were drowned in the attempt. On January 5th Captain Pierce ordered the helmsman to go about and seek shelter in Studland Bay. With only a jury rig, it was impossible to make much headway, and when darkness fell the *Halsewell* was approaching St Alban's Head and in danger of being swept into the race. The anchors were lowered, but dragged, and in the early hours of the 6th, the East Indiaman struck Seacombe Cliffs at a point about half-way between Winspit and Dancing Ledge, striking 'with such violence a shriek of horror burst at one instant from every quarter of the ship.'

Shortly afterwards, the ship broke its back, and those on board were either dragged under or flung into the water: 'Thus perished the *Halsewell*, and with her (went) worth, honour, skill, beauty, amiability and bright accomplishments.' Perhaps sixty people died when the ship foundered, amongst them Captain Pierce and all seven of the women. For those still alive the worst was yet to come. Many of the survivors had gathered in a cave at the base of the cliff, which though wet, afforded some refuge from the waves. During the night the cook and quartermaster managed to scale the 200 feet cliff and reach Eastington Farm, waking the steward to a local quarry-owner. The alarm was raised in Worth Matravers. Quarriers gathered on the cliff-top, first roping themselves together then beginning the task of hauling those trapped in the cave to safety. When dawn broke, the full extent of the disaster became visible. 'In the different recesses of the rocks,' wrote an eye-witness later, 'a confused heap of boats, broken masts, chests, trunks and dead bodies, were all huddled together, and the face of the water as far as the eye could extend, was disfigured with floating carcasses, tables, chairs, casks, and part of every other article in the vessel.'

The rescue work continued throughout the day. The quarriers were given two casks of spirits to sustain them, but some were 'more eager to drink themselves insensible than attend to the cries of the sufferers below', many of whom fell to their deaths. Others were washed from the rocks, and when the last of the survivors was finally lifted to safety nearly twenty-four hours after the *Halsewell* struck, the total death toll had risen to 166.

The wreck was not quickly forgotten. Tea-caddies depicting it were soon on sale to satisfy public curiosity. An account of the disaster, *A Circumstantial Narrative of the Loss of the Halsewell (East Indiaman), Captain Richard Pierce*, was written by the two chief-officers, Henry Meriton and John Rogers, and quickly ran to eight editions. Many years later Charles Dickens embellished the story for a minor and occasionally sentimental article in *Household Words*, entitled "The Long Voyage".

At the time, most attention was focused on the deaths of so many women and their reasons for being aboard. The press enjoyed the chance to teach morality – a quote from one newspaper should catch the flavour of all: 'It is a dreadful thing to hear of seven young ladies being drowned – nor is it much less lamentable to think that beautiful women are now reckoned among the articles of our export trade to India, not one ship is sailing now without a cargo on board; and they are literally going to market. On their arrival they are shewn as we show a horse, and are disposed of to the best bidder.'

Nor were the quarrymen forgotten. Later in the year, 100 guineas were distributed to those who had taken part in the rescue. But the final act was played out in December; for it was then that bills were posted announcing an auction at the Old Antelope Inn, Poole – 'being part of the cargo of the *Halsewell*, East Indiaman.'

St Alban's Head to Weymouth

When the mail steamship *Amazon* was destroyed by fire in the Bay of Biscay in 1852, much of the wreckage was washed up at Kimmeridge, driven there by the prevailing south-westerly wind and the unusual indraught that funnels into Kimmeridge Bay. Many ships owe their destruction to it, especially once dismasted or becalmed, but in reality it is merely one more peril on an already perilous coast.

West of St Alban's Head, the coastline abruptly gives way to a series of rocky ledges that extend seawards from the cliff face. Their resemblance to teeth could hardly be more appropriate, for once in their grip few ships have escaped. It was at Charnel, the aptly-named ledge east of Broad Bench, that the schooner *Liberty* was lost with all hands in 1868; near here that the ketch *Morning Star* with its cargo of copper broke up in 1906.

To list all the ships wrecked along the four miles of the Kimmeridge Ledges would perhaps be uncharitable. But Kimmeridge does not help its own cause, for it was in the Bay, following the beaching of the *Welfare* in 1371, that one of the most notorious of all Dorset shipwrecks occurred. The *Welfare* had run ashore during a storm, but was in no further danger when it fell victim to blatant abuse of Rights of Wreck, held at Kimmeridge by the Benedictine Abbey of Cerne. Once it was known that its cargo included silk and cloth-of-gold, the abbot's men deliberately forced the crew to abandon their ship – thus legally acquiring it for the abbot. A handful of minor gentry joined in the subsequent looting, and there was finally a commission of enquiry into the incident. For once even the Church was held accountable. Thomas, Abbot of Cerne, was found guilty of permitting buildings owned by the abbey to be used for storing stolen goods. One wonders how he would have reacted when the schooner *Gipsy Queen* struck the Ledges in 1878 laden with guano?

Many of the 19th century cargoes washed up at Kimmeridge suggest the stock of a Victorian emporium. The cargo of the 374 ton barque *Hardy*, wrecked on the Ledges in January 1861, included beer, hay, ladies' boots, ammunition, calico, 'brilliant kerchiefs for the Negro taste', sal ammonia, mirrors, Champagne, parasols, brandy and coal. The loss of the *Hardy* was perhaps inevitable, for it was outward bound for Africa in thick fog, commanded by a captain who had never navigated the Channel. It struck the Ledges 400 yards from the shore. The crew and passengers climbed into the boats and were soon lost. After nearly being swamped in St Alban's Race they were picked up by a passing schooner. In mid-morning the fog lifted, and the ship 'revealed herself to the astonished eyes of the coastguard on duty', with its cabin fire still alight.

Four years earlier the steamship *Tyne* had struck the same section of the Ledges. Once again fog was at fault, once again the cargo was remarkable. On board were fifty-five passengers, tapioca, cochineal, diamonds worth £32,548, and two lions. Unlike the *Hardy*, the *Tyne* was refloated, but by the time it had been towed off and refitted the bills totalled £25,000.

The destruction of the *Liberty* on Broad Bench in 1868 led to the opening of a permanent lifeboat station at Kimmeridge, for it had sunk with all hands before the local coastguards could offer assistance. The life-

The 600 ton Robert *on fire in Weymouth Bay before drifting ashore near St Alban's Head in 1847. The captain and crew of the American ship with its cargo of cotton had landed at Bridport.*

boat, the 28 feet five-oar *Mary Heape* arrived on station later that year, but its first service did not take place until four years later, when the Norwegian square-rigger *Stralsund* was wrecked in the Bay in December 1872. Waves were breaking on the Ledges, the wind was a gale force south-westerly, and it was only at the second attempt that the lifeboatmen were able to fire the rocket apparatus and take off the crew of seventeen.

The rocket apparatus was invaluable. The thirty-two people on board the French barque *Georgina*, driven on to the rocks in Chapman's Pool in 1866, owed their survival to a line fired from the shore. The same is true of the brigantine *Commodore*, wrecked in 1877 on Encombe Ledges, in poor visibility, when bound for Hamburg with a cargo of Welsh slate.

The changing character of the coasting trade and improvements in navigation have lessened the dangers of Lulworth, Worbarrow and Chapman's Pool. The most recent tragedy to have occurred in the area took place in December 1979 when the 36 feet yacht *Caroline of Leigh* foundered three miles off Lulworth with the loss of four lives. Chapman's Pool has not seen a wreck since the American 'Liberty' ship *T.A. Johnston* grounded in fog on Egmont Point in 1945. But the Kimmeridge Ledges remain as menacing as ever, and few years pass without some mishap taking place along their length.

Perhaps the most tragic disaster of recent years dates from January 1920 when the 5,500 ton *Treveal* was returning from Calcutta to Dundee with a cargo of jute and ore. It was without a pilot and sailing on a course that had been incorrectly laid. On the evening of the 9th it struck the Ledges half a mile from the shore. It remained there overnight awaiting the arrival of a tug, but due to a further error the tug never appeared. By morning the weather had changed. The decision was made to abandon ship. Both ships' boats capsized in the heavy seas and thirty-six lives were lost. It was a tragedy that need never have occurred. The Weymouth lifeboat *Friern Watch* was on its way; and on the following day, when the seas had calmed, it was discovered that the stern was intact and that the galley stove was still warm and the food untouched by the sea. Human negligence played its part, and the chief officer of the St Alban's Head Coastguard was later court-martialled and dismissed from his post. The *Treveal* continued causing damage even after the disaster.

The two sections of the 5,500 ton Treveal *after it had grounded on the Kimmeridge Ledges in 1920 with the loss of 36 lives.*

The first salvage vessel to attempt the removal of the cargo was holed by the wreck and sank, as did the steamer *Glenmore* when it struck the wreck in 1922.

To the crews of the sailing ships that once plied the coast, Weymouth Bay must have seemed safe enough after the dangers of Kimmeridge or Portland. But the sheer volume of shipping entering the Harbour made wrecks inevitable. In 1680 the pink *Agreement*, laden with buckskins and bearskins from the American Colonies, sank in the Harbour, blocking its mouth. Ships have foundered in full view of those walking on the Esplanade. When the revenue cutter *Hound* sunk opposite the Race Ground in about 1836, it was a further four years before the wreckage was washed ashore.

Apart from its commercial importance, Weymouth was also the headquarters of the local revenue service, harbouring the fast armed cutters crewed by the preventive officers in their war against smuggling. In

Weymouth lifeboat Friern Watch *drawing alongside the schooner* Ardente *after it had grounded in Weymouth Bay in December 1914. The five men on board were safely rescued.*

1770 one such cutter capsized whilst searching for smugglers and eight men were drowned. Tragedies like that must have shaken the town, but memories are short and the townsfolk wasted few opportunities to plunder. When the revenue smack *Weymouth* and the trader *Katherine* fell victim to the same storm in 1702 the combination proved irresistable. Untroubled and ignored, the locals helped themselves to the *Katherine*'s cargo of chestnuts. Finally some officers appeared, only to be 'beat and abused in the execution of their duties.' Other cargoes must have been equally welcome. The clove bark washed up when the 200 ton *Joanah* foundered in the Bay in 1707 may have had little attraction, but most of the wine on board the *La Notre Dame de Montaigne*, stranded near the town in 1701, is certain to have vanished into local cellars.

The Isle of Portland

On a Saturday in February 1717, a French coaster laden with wine was driven ashore in Chesil Cove. Customs officers tried to protect the cargo – and then the inevitable happened. 'Great numbers of . . . Portland Men came down upon us in Disguise Arm'd with Axes, Hatchetts, Clubbs, and beat us from the Goods wounding Severall of Us very much.' The officers' attempt to assist those on the ship met with the same response and they were forced to retreat, 'for fear of being knock'd on the Head with a Volley of Stones from the Islanders.'

Such incidents were once common on Portland. Most Portlanders regarded the plundering of wrecks as a birthright, a means of improving a way of life that brought hardship and poverty. Prior to the opening of the bridge to Wyke Regis in 1839 the Island was isolated from the rest of Dorset, nurturing self-sufficiency and an independence of spirit. There was scant grazing for livestock. The thin stony soil and the strip-system of farming kept yields small. The sea was a much richer larder, and more reliable, for until the advent of steam hardly a gale passed without a vessel ending its days on Portland.

The knowledge that the Island was approaching must have brought little comfort to mariners. Before the construction of the first lighthouse in 1716 the rounding of the Bill was always fraught with peril, for it meant avoiding Portland Race – the clash of tide and current that traditionally drove sailing vessels into the rocky coves on the west side of the Island. At spring tides the Race runs at 7 knots, and in an easterly gale, with an east-flowing stream, it can reach 10 knots and the whole area between the Bill and the Shambles is prone to overfalls and heavy breaking seas. Small vessels can safely hug the coast, but those without local knowledge round the Bill at their peril, especially if the wind veers to the south.

Beyond the Bill lies a second obstacle, the Shambles, the two miles of sand-bank that guards the southern approach into Weymouth Bay. It was here that the *Earl of Abergavenny* first struck in 1805, here that the 32 gun *Cormorant* grounded in 1762. In two places the depth reaches 11 feet at low tide, and there are many 16 feet shallows.

The loss of the *Earl of Abergavenny* is amongst the most tragic of all Dorset shipwrecks, and it has the unenviable distinction of costing more lives than any other Dorset disaster. The 1,200 ton East Indiaman weighed anchor off Portsmouth on February 1st 1805, bound for Bengal, where it was to load with cotton for sale in the Chinese port of Canton. Brokerage deals such as this were often profitable, and a successful voyage would have made a wealthy man out of the *Earl of Abergavenny*'s captain, John Wordsworth. But such a goal seems unlikely. His more celebrated brother, William, was the Poet Laureate. He himself was withdrawn and melancholic; characteristics which may have attracted him to the sea but which his crew mistook for wisdom and turned into a nickname, the 'Philosopher'.

The *Earl of Abergavenny*'s 164 man crew was substantial, but its tonnage and 30 guns made it the largest vessel in the Company service. In addition to the crew it carried 12 passengers, 180 newly recruited soldiers and 32 Chinamen. Also on board was a large quantity of Wedgewood china and a rumoured £70,000.

The 63 feet Lower Lighthouse on Portland after its construction in 1789. It was built to replace the original lighthouse of 1716.

The voyage seemed fated from the start. Indeed, when the final tragedy required explanation, much was made of the various portents and nautical superstitions that marked its progress: an accident when still in the Thames, the captain's moods, the remarkable link between the ship's naval escort, the frigate *Weymouth*, and its own final resting-place. Leaving Portsmouth, both the chief and third mates were left ashore and forced to give chase in a brig, an act of loyalty that was to cost Baggott, the chief mate, his life.

By Sunday February 3rd the weather had deteriorated, a strong south-westerly making headway difficult. Contact between the convoy and its escort had been lost. When dawn broke on the Tuesday the commodore gave the signal to run for shelter. The *Earl of Abergavenny* changed course for Portland

Roads, successfully taking on a pilot as it approached land. Later that afternoon, when the wind suddenly dropped, the East Indiaman struck the Shambles, hitting hard amongst the breakers.

If it was a pilot's incompetence that put the *Earl of Abergavenny* aground, it was undoubtedly Wordsworth's indecisiveness that laid the foundations for all that was to follow. The more one reads the published accounts of the disaster, the more striking seems Wordsworth's apparent indifference to both his own fate and that of his ship. The facts alone should have alerted him. It was midwinter. As darkness fell, the wind began rising again. A leak had been discovered and the bilges were filling with water. Yet the alarm had still to be given. No boats had been hoisted and no distress gun fired. When the ship finally refloated of its own accord and cleared the Shambles, Wordsworth first intended returning to Portsmouth for repairs. Only when Baggott announced that there was 12 feet of water in the holds did the gravity of the situation begin to lodge.

In the early evening, with the *Earl of Abergavenny* still sluggishly under-way but settling deeper in the water, the purser, third mate, and two of the three ladies on board set out for shore in the cutter, taking the ships' papers. A boat arrived from Weymouth and embarked the younger passengers. Soon a shoal of small boats had gathered round the doomed East Indiaman, but not one went alongside. Later, in their defence, the local boatmen argued that they were afraid their boats might be swamped by the sheer weight of numbers. Such excuses seem dubious. Accusations that they had gathered in hope of plunder remain all too probable.

Those on board were now aware of their danger. Panic was spreading. Apart from Baggott, most of the officers were more of a hindrance than a help. The crew had been issued with liquor in order to encourage them to man the pumps. No bribe could have been more disastrous. The more they laboured, the greater their thirst; the greater their drunkenness, the less their efficiency. Soon an armed guard was needed to keep the crew from breaking into the spirit-room.

Shortly before ten o'clock Baggott told his captain that there was no chance of saving the ship. Wordsworth replied, 'It cannot be helped; God's will be done.' An hour later the ship settled gently on to a sand-bank, eventually sliding into deeper water and leaving a section of the shrouds and some 25 feet of mainmast protruding above the waves. The survivors gathered in the rigging, but it was bitterly cold, and with the waves breaking over them, many soon fell into the sea. During the night a sloop braved the wreckage, drawing close enough to take off the survivors. In all, 233 men and one woman died that night, making it the most costly of Dorset wrecks and certainly the most unnecessary. Its author, John Wordsworth, was last seen clinging to a rope. He refused to accept help, and on March 20th his body was found washed up on the beach near Weymouth: he was buried at Wyke Regis. Later that spring his brother William walked the track from Grasmere to Paterdale and composed a poem in his memory. It begins with a description of a buzzard in flight, and continues:

> Oh! could he on that woeful night
> Have lent his wing, my Brother Dear,
> For one poor moment's space to Thee,
> And all who struggled with the Sea,
> When safety was so near.

There were the inevitable post-mortems; the usual pamphlets giving 'An Authentic Narrative' of the East Indiaman's loss; the by now traditional auction of all that had been salvaged from the wreck (part of its rudder provided a staircase for a Weymouth house). And for the next few summers, anyone training a telescope out to sea on a spot 2½ miles south-south-east of Weymouth Esplanade, might have seen divers being lowered into the water in search of the coins thought to have been on the ship when it foundered.

There is no memorial to those who drowned on the *Earl of Abergavenny*, but another celebrated Dorset shipwreck is today remembered by the small church at South-

An inaccurate but dramatic illustration showing the Earl of Abergavenny *foundering in Weymouth Bay in February 1805.*

well on Portland that bears the name of one of the two ships involved.

In September 1877 the 1,154 ton iron sailing ship *Avalanche* was sailing down Channel, outward bound for New Zealand with a crew of thirty-four and sixty-three emigrants on board. Sailing towards it was the slightly larger wooden-built *Forest*, bound in ballast with a crew of twenty-one under Captain Lockhart.

On the night of Tuesday the 11th, in driving rain and with the weather worsening, a ship's light was spotted by the helmsman on the *Forest*. Lockhart checked his own lights, but thought further action unnecessary. Moments later, when evasion was impossible, the *Forest* struck the *Avalanche* amidships, almost cutting it in two. The *Avalanche* 'staggered violently, gave three plunges, and then went down like a piece of lead, carrying all on board with her.' Within four minutes of striking, it had vanished. Most of the passengers were drowned in their beds. The only survivors were the third mate and two seamen who scrambled on to the bows of the *Forest* as the ship went down.

For those on the *Forest*, the worst was yet to come. The blow had caused serious damage and it was shipping water. Certain that his ship would soon share the *Avalanche*'s fate, Lockhart gave orders to abandon ship. It was dark, his shaken crew was composed of seven nationalities. In the confusion that followed, three boats were launched, but an attempt to pick up some of the crew who had been accidentally left on board failed. During the night one boat foundered and was never seen again. A second capsized and was later washed up on the Chesil.

Early next morning four corpses were

Two Portland lerrets bringing ashore the survivors from the Avalanche *and* Forest *after their collision off Portland in September 1877.*

found ashore on Portland. Shortly afterwards the third boat was spotted two miles off-shore in danger of foundering. Two lerrets were launched through the breakers, manned by fourteen fishermen. 'For those stout hearts and strong arms the tempest tossed billows of the West Bay had no terrors.' They returned with the twelve survivors of the collision, an act of heroism that completely contradicts the tales of plunder normally associated with all Portlanders.

The tragedy was not quickly forgotten.

The *Forest* refused to sink, and an attempt to blow it up merely shifted the ballast and left its bows touching sand and 40 feet of stern sticking out of the water. The Weymouth & Portland Steam Packet Co. staged special trips to witness the antics of *HMS Defense* as it struggled to sink the wreck. Rather than endure the ridicule, its captain decided to tow the *Forest* down Channel, finally destroying it with explosives.

Six corpses had by then been found and buried. By law, bodies washed ashore became the responsibility of the parish overseer; but the lack of ceremony at the service reached the notice of *The Times*, who in turn publicized the funeral and condemned the 'hasty and shameful treatment of the dead' and the use of a 'common four wheel wagon drawn by a black and white horse' for carrying the coffins. An inquest followed, with the coroner and rector of Portland both manoeuvring to shift the blame on to the other. The publicity led to the friends and relatives of the dead deciding to build a memorial church. A site was purchased in Southwell near the cliff, facing the scene of the collision, and the Church of St Andrew is now commonly known as Avalanche Church. Nor were the fishermen forgotten. The *Forest*'s ships' boats were given to them, as were various testimonials and awards. Perhaps most welcome (for no ship's boat could match the efficiency of a lerret) was the £140 that was divided between them.

Collisions off Portland were all too frequent as the shipping lanes grew busier. A year earlier, a Jersey schooner, the *Annie Edwin*, had sunk after striking a Norwegian brig during the night. In 1866 the 1,000 ton naval sloop *Amazon* collided with the steamship *Osprey*, which instantly sank with the loss of ten lives. In June 1883 there was yet another collision, and once again New Zealand interests were involved. The *Waitara* and *Hurunui* were both iron-built square-riggers of the New Zealand Shipping Co. sailing in convoy for Wellington. On the evening of the 22nd they were sailing in slight mist on opposite tacks. Suddenly it became apparent that due to errors by the two captains the two ships were on a collision course. The *Hurunui* hit the *Waitara* amidships, recoiled slightly, then struck again – driven forward by the wind in its sails. Two minutes later the *Waitara* had sunk with the loss of twenty-six lives, amongst them a stowaway. Nearly sixty years earlier, in 1826, the mail packet *Francis Feeling* was run down by a Swedish brig with the loss of all ten members of the crew, leaving thirty children fatherless.

The establishment of the packet service between Weymouth and the Channel Islands in 1794 had made such calamities inevitable. Four years later, in 1830, the packet paddle-steamer *Meteor* ran on to the rocks at Church Ope Cove in thick fog. Its arrival met with a characteristic response, for it had soon been looted.

At times it may seem that the pleasures of plundering were indigenous to Portland. But Purbeck was as guilty, as were the villages stretched along the Chesil. Its pedigree is ancient, for the first Portland wreck to be accurately dated occurred in 1305, when a Spanish ship was wrecked on the Isle. 'As the worn out mariners transferred themselves to shore alive, Henry Blake and about 200 others, all named, entered the ship, carried away the goods, broke the ship and cut it to pieces.' Six years later another Spanish ship enjoyed a similar fate, though in this instance the wrecking was deliberate. The wine laden *Sainte Goymelote* was sheltering from a storm when it was boarded by a group of Portlanders. Its cable was cut and the wind drove it ashore, where the waiting crowds then emptied it of its cargo.

Plundering was not without risk, and by the mid-18th century those who engaged in it were liable to transportation. From 1713, the statute against wrecking and plundering was read aloud in all coastal churches four times a year. Such deterrents had little effect. The potential rewards made the risks acceptable, and fostered endless ingenuity. When in October 1778 customs officers placed the brandy from the wrecked French sloop *La Bien-Aime* in a locked building on Portland, they must have considered it safe. But the building was thatched, and when they next returned, the thatch had been cut and much of the brandy had vanished. In 1762 a Cornish vessel foundered off Portland. Its cargo of brandy was retrieved by customs officers. Some Portlanders then seized the casks from their legal custodians and threw them back into the sea. Boats were launched, and the casks were weighted with stones so that they could be collected at a later date. Five years later it was the turn of the *Peggy*, London bound from New England with a cargo of mahogany and whale oil, and gold from the London Custom's House. The chance discovery of some coins and the lid of a bullion chest was adequate bait, and soon an armada of small boats was 'Creeping where the ship was lost.'

The efficiency of the revenue service and a changing attitude to plundering led to its gradual reduction. But change and progress did not halt the tally of shipwrecks, and even the laying of the first stone of Portland Breakwater by Prince Albert in 1849 brought mixed blessings to the ships it was designed to protect. Accidents to stone barges were frequent. In 1869, shortly before the completion of the first two moles, three vessels were wrecked on the Breakwater. In 1910, after the completion of another two miles of mole, the coal hulk *Haytian* was rammed and sunk in the Harbour: after being raised in 1937 it was rammed again, and again it sank. Such misfortunes seem to dog certain ships. In 1922 the oil tanker *Scandinavia* sank after striking the Breakwater. In the following April the salvage vessel *Freewill* was wrecked whilst trying to salvage the *Scandinavia*.

Other accidents in the Harbour have been rather more tragic. In October 1948, a 'Liberty' boat from *HMS Illustrious* capsized in a storm and twenty-nine sailors were drowned. Seven years later the submarine

The Greek steamer Preveza *after it grounded on the Chesil in January 1930 in thick fog. Attempts to tow it off failed when the towing tug's anchor chain got caught in its own propellor, and after a two day storm the* Preveza *had broken in two.*

The ill-fated coal hulk Haytian *after it had been rammed in Portland Harbour in July 1910.*

Sidon sank after an explosion in the torpedo bay, thirteen lives were lost. The expansion of Portland as a naval base has made tragedy all too common. In January 1924, when the Atlantic Fleet sailed from the Harbour, the submarine *L-24* sank west of the Bill after a collision with *HMS Resolution*. Forty-three lives were lost, and there is a plaque to the dead in St Anne's Church, Portsmouth Dockyard. Two other submarines also collided on the same day and the battleship *Ramillies* struck the Breakwater. In 1932 the submarine *M2* failed to resurface after a training dive three miles west of the Bill, there were no survivors. Its loss was unusual, for it carried a seaplane that was launched by catapult, and it now seems certain that the hanger doors were not fully watertight.

Despite such disasters, Portland has played host to a whole series of wrecks where lives have been inexplicably spared. The paddle-steamer *Bournemouth* was returning from an excursion trip to Torquay when it struck near the Bill in thick fog in 1886. It was travelling at full speed, had 194 people on board and only one lifeboat. But although the steamer was finally wrecked, the sea was calm, there was no panic, and no lives were lost. Curiously, for it has the reputation of being a graveyard for shipping, the most remarkable of such incidents are all associated with Blacknor Point. In 1907 the 5,500 ton steamer *Patroclus* was stranded on the Point, but was towed to safety a week later. Three years later the German steamer *Okahandja* was also towed off after running aground in fog. The German liner *Bulow* was another potential casualty of fog that was refloated undamaged after striking the Point. And in February 1936 the residents of Weston woke to find the 35,000 ton Union Castle liner *Winchester Castle* aground on the Point. It also survived, and was successfully refloated.

The German steamer Okahandja *on Blacknor Point in June 1910. Much of the cargo had to be jettisoned before the steamer could be refloated.*

◁*The paddle-steamer* Bournemouth *prior to breaking up near Portland Bill after it had struck the rocks in thick fog in 1886.*

△*The German liner* Bulow *on Blacknor Point in June 1914.*

The Chesil Beach

In his novel *Moonfleet*, first published in 1898 and now rightly regarded as a classic adventure story, J. Meade Falkner wrote of a shipwreck on the Chesil:

> And once on the beach, the sea has little mercy, for the water is deep right in, and the waves curl over and fall on the pebbles with a weight no timbers can withstand. Then if the poor fellows try to save themselves, there is a deadly under-tow or rush back of the water, which sucks them off their legs, and carries them again under the thundering waves.'

As a recital of what actually happens to those wrecked on the Chesil, that description cannot be bettered. For the eighteen mile bank of pebbles bounds the cruellest lee-shore in Dorset. To the west, it ends beneath the 200 feet cliffs of West Bay; to the east, in the more appropriately named Dead Man's Bay. The Beach is at its most lethal in a south-westerly, and once embayed and certain of striking, a prudent captain would order his helmsman to run hard ashore in hope of grounding as high as possible on the bank: only then might his crew scramble on to the pebbles and escape the undertow.

Early wrecks along its length have all the hall-marks of those on Portland, and as high a death toll. In December 1641 the schooner *Golden Grape* was driven ashore near Wyke and seven of the twenty men on board were drowned. It took three days to break up, by which time the local villagers had begun loading its cargo of raisins, silk, wine, oil and bullion on to carts and pack-horses. A century later, in January 1749, the only true treasure ship to have been wrecked off Dorset struck opposite Fleet, causing scenes of looting unparalleled in the county's history.

The 350 ton Dutch merchantman *Hope* was returning to Amsterdam from Curacao when thick fog and high winds blew it off course. On board was £50,000 in bullion, much of it silver and gold dust. We may condemn the events that followed, but they have an atmosphere of wildness and lawlessness that hints at some more rumbustious age. The *Hope* struck the Beach on the night of January 16th, quickly breaking into three pieces. No light was visible from the lighthouse, a failing that was later judiciously blamed on 'intense mists and the particular fogginess of the air.' The mast snapped and fell on the shore, allowing the crew of seventy-four to climb precariously to safety. The hull soon rolled back into the sea and was never seen again. But the fore-deck was washed ashore, and the cabin (containing most of the bullion) was buried beneath flotsam and pebbles. The first plunderers arrived at dawn, the probable discovery of some of the bullion feeding the appetite of the gathering crowd. Clubs, scythes and cutlasses were used to threaten the unfortunate Dutchmen; all of whom must have been dazed and shocked as they huddled on the Beach, unfed, still wet, and in a foreign country: at a trial later, the counsel for the crown called them 'A poor, feeble, miserable company of strangers, almost naked, shuddering with cold, sinking under the want of the necessary supports of life, their limbs all sodden and drench'd by the briny waters . . .'

The crowd grew, becoming so large that it was organized into gangs, who roamed the Beach wearing differing colours to identify the villages from which they had come. At one point it was estimated that in excess of 10,000 people, from throughout Dorset, had

The Norwegian barque Patria *in the process of being destroyed on the Chesil in October 1903. The crew was taken off by rocket line.*

gathered in search of plunder. When spirits appeared amidst the wreckage, looting surrendered to drunkenness. Some died from exposure. One man was stabbed to death and hastily buried in a shallow grave on the Beach. Village squabbled with village over possession of the bullion and baled cloth carried by the *Hope*.

No such orgy could last indefinitely. Ten days after the *Hope* broke up, the local justices, supported by troops, dispersed the mob and cleared the Beach. During the weeks that followed house to house searches throughout Portland and Wyke Regis led to the recovery of much of the bullion.

At the Dorchester Summer Assizes in July, Augustin Elliot, a Portlander, was tried for the theft of ten ounces of gold and twenty of silver. Not unexpectedly he was acquitted, for those on the jury were as guilty as he. When questioned as to why he had made no attempt to stop the looting, Bartholomew Cooper, excise officer on Portland, gave an answer that both sums up those ten days of anarchy and remains a masterpiece of irrelevancy and evasion: 'Early Monday morning I heard a loud talking in Chesil . . . that a ship was on shore. I got up, but the thing being doubtful, I went and fed my horse with oats at a stable which was at some distance.' Faced by such replies, the judge accepted defeat and dismissed all further cases connected with the *Hope*.

Five years later, in December 1754, Thomas Francklyn, rector of Langton-Herring and vicar of Fleet, preached a sermon attacking the looting that took place on the Chesil whenever a ship went down. Its appeal must have been wide, for it was later published as a pamphlet under the title *Serious Advice and Fair Warning To all that live upon the Sea-Coast of England and Wales, particularly to those in the Neighbourhood of Weymouth and Portland*.

Whatever the promises of repentance inspired by Francklyn's words, they were soon forgotten. In January 1762 the French privateer *Zenobie* was wrecked on the Chesil opposite the Ferry House (its position is shown on Isaac Taylor's map of 1765): eight men were drowned, two of whom were swept off the Beach. But the seventy-one survivors were robbed and then stripped of their clothes, treatment that so angered George III, that although England and France were at war, he ordered them to be sent back to France rather than be kept as prisoners.

Thirty years after Taylor had drawn his map of the county, a group of militia were patrolling the Chesil at daybreak on November 18th 1795 when they saw a merchantman strike near the Ferry House. That first glimpse of the *Aeolus* marked the start of the worst disaster ever known on the Chesil, and once again the behaviour of the local villagers was marred by looting.

Three days earlier, a convoy of merchantmen and military transports, escorted by a squadron under Admiral Hugh Christian, had set sail from the Solent for the West Indies. The transports were crammed with soldiers joining an expedition under Sir Ralph Abercrombie. The wind shifted off Torbay, and the fleet was soon confronted by a south-south-westerly gale. Christian signalled his ships to take shelter, but fog forced him to give a second signal ordering the fleet to stand out to sea. The fleet soon broke up, many of the vessels being driven eastward by the wind. The combination of fog and high winds was unusual, but for six of the ships under Christian's command it meant failure to clear Portland and their final destruction on the Chesil. Others were lost off Plymouth, and even some of those that successfully rounded the Bill later foundered off the Isle of Wight.

The *Aeolus* was the first ashore, and nine men were drowned when they unwisely plunged into the breakers. But the nine who remained on board survived, saved by a succession of immense waves that tossed the merchantman with its cargo of timber, masts and military stores high on to the pebbles. Shortly afterwards a second merchantman, the *Golden Grove*, was driven ashore nearby, and although there were eighteen survivors, a further five lives were lost.

Such losses seem small when measured against the disaster simultaneously taking place four miles to the west, between Fleet and Chickerell. For it was there that another merchant ship, the *Thomas*, and three military transports, the *Catherine*, *Venus* and *Piedmont*, were all wrecked. The facts underline the extent of the tragedy. Of those on the *Thomas* thirteen were drowned and sixteen saved. Eighteen survived from the *Piedmont*, out of a complement of 157. A further eighteen survived on the *Venus*, but ninety-two were drowned. The losses on the *Catherine* totalled forty men and twenty-eight horses, and the sole survivors were a Mrs. Burns and the ship's boy. In all, the Chesil claimed 298 lives from the six vessels.

The pregnant Mrs. Burns later gave an account of the last moments on board the *Catherine*. 'The passengers and soldiers seemed thunderstruck by the sense of immediate and inevitable danger; and the seamen, too, conscious of the hopelessness of any extertion, stood in speechless agony, certain of meeting the destruction which now menaced them.' Her own escape was remarkable. Resisting the urge to return to her cabin and await death, she was thrown into the surf when the ship struck. Those on the beach made no attempt to save her, and a rogue wave finally tossed her on to the pebbles. Others were ignored as well. An officer who had been thrown ashore was about to be robbed when a chest was washed up alongside him. He was forgotten, to be swept back into the breakers whilst 'the inhuman wretches' began bickering over the chest. By noon, two miles of beach 'were strewn with the dead bodies of men and animals, with fragments of wreck and piles of plundered goods, around which groups of the natives were busily thieving.'

Yet for once there is some evidence that contradicts the accusations of plundering. William Lloyd, master of the *Aeolus*, in a letter published later, stated that the survivors from his ship enjoyed 'the most hospitable treatment we could have experienced in

One of only two survivors from the Catherine, *Mrs Burns, after six ships of Admiral Christian's squadron had struck on the Chesil in 1795.*

any part of the world', and that the Portlanders 'actually hazarded their lives to preserve those who were in danger.' For the dead such arguments did not matter. The officers and women were buried in Wyke churchyard, the rest in unmarked common graves on the inner shore.

The common grave was often employed, mainly because of lack of space in already crowded graveyards. On Easter Monday, March 27th 1815, the East Indiaman *Alexander*, returning from Bombay with a cargo of cotton, sugar, coffee, pepper and rice, was wrecked near Wyke. Of the 160 passengers and crew there were only five survivors (four lascars and a woman), and sixty of the dead were buried in a single grave near the south gate of St George's, Portland. One casualty was a Lady Jackson, returning from India with her children. Her body was washed up at Lyme Regis, where it was daily strewn with fresh flowers by the fossilist Mary Anning. The cargo vanished without trace, and all that was salvaged from the wreck was a packet of letters addressed to the governors of the East India Company. Nothing is known of the behaviour of the local villagers, but when the Swedish brig *Iris* struck on the Chesil seven years later five of the crew were saved thanks to the 'active and humane exertions of the Portland seamen, who, to their honour, are ever ready on these melancholy occasions to risk their own lives to save those of their fellow human beings.'

The *Alexander* had been at sea for nearly five months when it foundered, and an equally long voyage lay ahead for those on board the 1,385 ton *Royal Adelaide* when it set sail for Australia in November 1872. But the iron-built clipper with its crew of thirty and thirty-nine emigrants never completed its voyage, and its destruction on the Chesil is still remembered over a century later. The reasons bring little honour to Dorset. For it was the last occasion when the county engaged in wholesale looting, and the numbers who died from drunkenness were nearly as great as those who went down with the ship.

The *Royal Adelaide* had turned back to seek shelter from a south-westerly gale when in passage down Channel. It was spotted struggling to round Portland Bill, and a blue light was lit in Chesil Cove to indicate where it was safest to attempt running hard on to the Beach. The captain was unaware of his position, later admitting that he thought he had cleared the Shambles and was off Lul-

A group photograph of all the men who survived the wreck of the Royal Adelaide.

worth. Anchors were lowered to help slow the pace and keep it clear of the Beach, but they dragged. Late that night it struck opposite Ferry Bridge, rolling broadside to the Beach in the breakers – where no one could reach it. The first mate drowned trying to swim ashore with a line. The rocket apparatus was set up, and a group of Portlanders, linked by ropes, successfully tossed a line aboard. About sixty people were taken off, then the line snapped. The handful of men and women left huddled on the poop of the clipper were washed away during the night, and by morning it had broken up and sunk off the Chesil, where a section of it still remains.

And there the disaster might have ended – yet one more wreck on an already lengthy list. But as the *Royal Adelaide* broke up, the cargo was washed ashore. Hats, soap, candles, cotton, coffee, sugar and livestock (a solitary pig survived) poured from its holds. But most eagerly awaited by those watching were the casks of brandy, rum and cheap Dutch gin that began to appear amongst the flotsam. In the words of a contemporary poem by a Portland quarryman:

But while some were plundering and carrying
 things home,
Others were busy in drinking the rum,
While some with pebbles soon knocked the head
 in,
Of the big brandy tubs and casks of gin;
For they felt themselves cold and thought it no
 harm,
To have a good drink to keep themselves warm.
But alas! poor souls, they drank rather too deep
Of the brandy and rum – then soon fell asleep
In the wind and the rain, to lie all the night,
In a drunken state, and an awful plight;

Accounts differ as to the final death toll. Seven went down with the *Royal Adelaide* itself, but as many as five may have died from drunkenness followed by exposure. Men were seen burying their spoils beneath the shingle, others risked drowning to drag the casks from the surf. The crowd was estimated at 3,000, and with masterly understatement the *Dorset County Chronicle* later remarked that 'the scene which met their view must have amply repaid them.'

Bridport to Lyme Regis

The perils facing shipping crossing Lyme Bay lessen once the Chesil lies astern. Start Point is the next landfall, the open Channel and broadening sea lanes make collision less likely. But for those employed on the schooners and ketches that once served the Channel ports, Dorset's two most formidable harbour entrances still lay ahead. Both are man made, and both owe their existence to the demands of commerce.

Bridport Harbour is now known as West Bay, a name foisted on it by the Great Western Railway when the line to the Harbour was opened in 1884. To the medieval mariner it was simply Bridport Haven, or Creek – the name associated with its earliest recorded wrecks. Most such wrecks were of ships bound for Lyme Regis, then the sole anchorage between Portland Roads and Exmouth, and a major part trading wool for French wines. In 1670 a Lyme barque carrying salt was cast up near Bridport with the loss of two lives; two other Lyme ships were lost in the same storm.

Bridport's gradual expansion into the centre of the netting and marine cordage industries led to the improvement of the Harbour. In the mid-18th century the River Brit was diverted and the first piers and wharves were constructed, initially out of oak. It remains an unlikely site for a harbour. Self-interest may explain its description as a 'safe port wherein may ride some 40 sail', but that is far from the truth. It is neither easy to enter nor easy to leave. The piers are 60 feet apart. The approach channel is narrow and troubled by a sand bar. In strong onshore winds, particularly a south-westerly, it could not be entered at all and ships moored off risked destruction under the cliffs to the east.

In fair winds, ships due to dock anchored off whilst awaiting the tide. Such patience was not always possible. The Bridport registered *Marie Leocadie* was returning from South Shields with coal in 1868 when it began shipping water in worsening weather. Its master was forced to choose between sinking at sea or risking running aground on the sand bar. He chose the latter, with predictable results. Once aground, the *Marie Leocadie* soon began breaking up, blocking the harbour mouth and bringing the port to a standstill for two weeks. Another victim of adverse winds was the ketch *Olive*, becalmed in January 1895, and eventually holed when it drifted with the tide on to the piles abutting the pier. Despite its loss, there would have been no casualties had a fisherman not been drowned trying to board it on the following day. Shipwrecks tempt such tragedies. They attract crowds, encouraging a carelessness that the sea is quick to punish. In 1869 a member of the Gundry family was drowned whilst watching the brigantine *Demetrius* break up on the shingle.

Another well-known local wreck is that of the iron-built *Alioth*, the victim of the miserliness of its captain and now a snag for fishermen. After docking in West Bay in April 1923 with a cargo of Swedish timber, the *Alioth* had reloaded with sand, but was prevented from sailing by a southerly wind. A local boat offered to tow it out to sea far enough for it to clear Portland Bill (then a common practice), but its German captain refused to part with the 10/- fee. An attempt to push it clear of the piers using boat hooks

The final destruction of the Alioth *at West Bay in April 1923.*

ended in disaster when it ran aground before the wind had filled the sails. In the weeks that followed it defied all efforts to refloat it, finally heeling on to its side and breaking up when gales swept the coast.

Two other Bridport wrecks deserve mention. The first occurred in 1865 when the schooner *Black Diamond* was wrecked on the beach with a cargo of Irish oats, destined for the Bull Hotel. Five years later, a second schooner, the *Kennet*, was lost on the same part of the beach whilst carrying an identical cargo for the same hotel.

Many Dorset shipwrecks took place at night or out of sight of land. Occasionally the timbers bearing their names were destroyed or never recovered, making identification impossible. Usually such ships were foreign, and the uncertainty surrounding their loss must have meant an agonizing wait for the families of their crews. In the gales at the end of January 1817 an unidentified French chasse-marée with a cargo of wine was lost with all hands on Charmouth Beach, and a second nameless French vessel was seen to founder off Abbotsbury. Those same January gales claimed other victims. The *Trois Amis* of Bordeaux was lost approaching Bridport. At Lyme Regis, the *Volante*, *Mary* and *Union* were all wrecked in the storm that destroyed the Cobb.

The damage to the Cobb must have caused temporary hardship in the town. For it was Lyme's life-line, the bulwark against the sea that had brought the town its wealth and given it a Custom House. In westerly and southerly gales it offered refuge to vessels crossing Lyme Bay: those that failed to reach it were traditionally washed under the neighbouring cliffs. Wrecks must have been commonplace. Fifty ships are thought to have been lost in November 1377 when storms caused havoc in the town. The first wreck that can be named dates from 1709 when a six-rater, the 24 gun *HMS Solebay* broke up on the rocks. Forty years later, in 1748, the Spanish ship *Laguiticus de Lille*

Dieu suffered a similar fate. Its cargo of wool was lost, but thanks to 'the care and diligence of the people on the shore the crew were all saved.' Not all wrecks have ended so satisfactorily. In December 1836 a coastguard cutter commanded by John Keogh saved four of the five men on board the schooner *William & Ann*, but Keogh was later drowned attempting to salvage its stores and awarded a posthumous silver medal by the Royal Institution for the Preservation of Lives from Shipwreck.

A second silver medal was awarded to Lyme when the barque *Heroine* struck the rocks close to the Cobb on Boxing Day 1852. The *Heroine* was outward bound for Australia with emigrants when it ran into a south-westerly gale. The two ships' boats were lowered and all forty-five people on board reached safety. But a pinnace from the revenue cruiser *Frances* had been launched to help guide the boats through the surf, and it was the pinnace that proved the less seaworthy. It capsized in the surf, with the loss of four lives. A fund was started for the families of the dead, and the silver medal was awarded to the sole survivor, William Bridle.

The need for a lifeboat at Lyme Regis had long been known, but the events following the wreck of the *Heroine* accelerated its arrival. The 27 feet eight-oared self-righter appeared in September 1853 and was initially housed in a shed beneath a sail loft. It was soon in use, for on the following New Year's Day the French brigantine *Jeune Rose* was spotted about five miles out flying its distress flag. The lifeboat was launched into a south-westerly gale, but successfully reached the crippled ship. Tragically, the *Jeune Rose* partially rolled over when its cargo shifted, and the change of weight was sufficient to capsize the lifeboat as it lay alongside. Three of the coastguards were trapped in the air pocket beneath it, one of whom died before it could be righted.

In 1903 the railway reached Lyme Regis, ending its career as a port. To many it must have seemed that the reduction in shipping would mean a similar reduction in the number of shipwrecks – and in the loss of local lives. But the 20th century has not proved so charitable. In March 1918 the steamship *Baygitano* was torpedoed 1½ miles south-west of the town: three men were killed, five rescued by lifeboat. Three months later the steamship *Moidart* was torpedoed seven miles south-west of the town with the loss of fifteen lives. But the war-time wreck most associated with the

The 15,000 ton battleship Formidable, *torpedoed in Lyme Bay on New Year's Day 1915 with the loss of 551 lives.*

Lassie, the cross-bred collie responsible for saving the life of a seaman after the loss of the Formidable.

town is surely that of the battleship *Formidable*, torpedoed in the Bay on New Year's Day 1915.

The 15,000 ton battleship was serving the Channel Fleet as part of the 5th Battle Squadron under the command of Vice Admiral Sir Lewis Bayly. Its loss remains controversial. When torpedoed, it was without a destroyer screen and the squadron was sailing in line ahead, making it a perfect submariner's target. Rescue attempts were hampered by bad weather, and out of a ship's complement of 750 there were only 199 survivors. Some were picked up by a cruiser serving with the squadron, others by a fishing smack that had nearly run down one of the two ship's cutters to be successfully launched. The fate of the second cutter remained unresolved until dusk on the following evening, when cries were heard off Lyme Regis beach. The cutter had grounded in the surf, on board were fifty survivors from the *Formidable*, nine of whom were later to die. It was the first major naval disaster of the war, and for his 'want of prudence and good seamanship' Bayly was removed from his command.

One of the survivors washed up at Lyme deserves a historical foot-note. Amongst those rescued and supposedly lying dead on the floor of the Pilot Boat Inn was A.B. John Cowan, and it was only realized that Cowan was alive after he had been licked for about half-an-hour by the landlord's rough-haired cross-bred collie, Lassie. Reports of the incident reached Hollywood, inspiring the creation of the now immortal sheepdog that still bears Lassie's name. A second dog links Dorset with the *Formidable*. Captain Loxley's terrier, Bruce, lies buried in Abbotsbury churchyard.

The 'Great Gale'

Like the shipwrecks they cause, some storms acquire a reputation that lives on when others are forgotten. History remembers them, they become the yardstick by which their successors are measured. The events of the night of Monday November 23rd 1824 belong to that company.

The 'Great Gale', as that storm is now known, was a gale of classic simplicity, a marriage of wind and tide that swept the entire Channel coast and caused damage wherever it touched. Human error played little part in it. The seaworthiness of the ships involved and the ability of their crews can be ignored. As one contemporary newspaper remarked, 'it threatened terror to the most sheltered head, and awakened awe in the most callous heart.' The passage of time has not softened that description. The 'Great Gale' is now part of Dorset folk-lore, remembered as the cause of the destruction of Fleet church and as marking the only occasion a vessel was swept so high on to the Chesil that it was relaunched in Portland Roads.

The wind began freshening on the previous day, turning south-south-west as it strengthened. By Monday evening it had reached Storm Force and the spring tide had turned. That evening the 100 ton *Hero*, laden with stone from Swanage, foundered off Hengistbury Head with the loss of four lives. The tide reached the high-water mark during the night, but kept rising, flooding Poole Quay and breaking and dragging moorings.

Weymouth fared no better. The gale struck the town at 4 a.m., and when dawn broke on the Tuesday the pier had been partly demolished, the quay and many houses were flooded, and the once elegant Esplanade with its neat chain-linked posts had been destroyed. In the Bay it was the shipping that suffered. The *Louisa*, an Exeter smack, foundered with the loss of two lives. Opposite Osmington Mills, a second smack, the *Sally*, capsized, and all on board were drowned except the captain's son who leapt on board the local brig *Nancy* before the *Sally* went down. The *Nancy* itself, though dismasted, successfully rode out the gale in Portland Roads. A larger vessel, of about 500 tons, was seen to founder in the Bay, but its name remains unknown. Others were more fortunate. A Swedish vessel rode out the gale in Chesil Cove with its masts cut away. The Dutch galliot, *Johanna Christina*, outward bound from Rotterdam to Bordeaux with a cargo of cheeses, struck on the rocks below Sandsfoot Castle, and although the galliot was destroyed the crew were able to scramble to safety.

For those unfortunate enough to be caught off Portland and the Chesil there could be no such miracle. Nor was the safety of land any guarantee of immunity. The tide was so high and the waves were so steep that the sea breached the Chesil. The village of Chiswell was the hardest hit. Thirty people were drowned and nearly a hundred houses were flooded or destroyed. The Ferry House at Smallmouth shared their fate, and 'the poor, honest, worthy old ferryman, after 30 years service fell a victim to his own benevolence' – he was drowned attempting to save a soldier and his horse. The *Colville*, West Indiaman, foundered in West Bay and its crew was 'consigned to a watery grave.' One of the passengers, Henry Gosling, cut a

A drawing by Carter Galpin showing the wreck of the Unity *between Lyme Regis and Charmouth during the 'Great Gale' of November 1824.*

piece from his shirt, wrote his name on it, and tied it round his neck so that his corpse could be identified and his family informed. In all, seventeen bodies were later washed ashore and buried on Portland: some wine, rum and fifteen bales of cotton was all that was saved of the cargo. Another West Indiaman, the *Carvalho*, again laden with rum and cotton, was also lost off the Chesil and all on board it were drowned.

A third vessel that must have seemed doomed to those watching was the government sloop *Ebenezer*, on route between Portsmouth and Plymouth with military stores. But the *Ebenezer* survived, for although its master was drowned, his ship was washed so high on to the Chesil that the crew were able to jump to safety. The sloop was later dragged over the summit of the Beach and relaunched into Portland Roads: the only ship known to have done so.

Further west the dangers were as great. A Danish brig laden with fruit struck near Abbotsbury with the loss of four lives. Altogether over a hundred bodies were washed ashore between Bexington and Swyre in the three days following the gale. It is probable that some would have been buried in Fleet churchyard, but that too fell victim to what one newspaper described as a 'tempest heavy with . . . frightful terrors'. The sea broached the East Fleet, flooding the village, and all that now remains of the old parish church is its chancel. Nor did Bridport escape. The sloops *Bee* and *Lively*, the schooner *Fram* and a new unnamed vessel were carried over the Quay walls.

Only at Lyme does human folly compound the tragedy. If the government had been less spendthrift in its attitude to repairing the Cobb in the wake of the storms of 1817, many of the ships destroyed seven years later might have survived. The shortsightedness took its toll. Waves breached the Harbour wall and the revenue cruiser *Fox* broke its moorings, sinking opposite the

Assembly Rooms: the two preventive officers who died left a total of eleven children. A fishing smack, the 16 ton *Caroline*, was carried up the Buddle and wedged beneath the bridge, where it soon broke up. Another vessel, the *Eliza*, was also lost. A smack sitting on the stocks in the shipbuilding yard awaiting its launching ceremony, due to be held on the following day, found itself launched prematurely – and simultaneously wrecked.

But two ships survived. The *Mary & Elizabeth*, which had thrice turned back from Guernsey with its cargo of sail-cloth because of the weather, was stranded near Church Cliffs and later relaunched; as was the London trader, *Unity*, based at Lyme. The *Unity* might have weathered the storm had not the bollard to which it was tied broken away when a section of the Cobb wall collapsed. The crew were on board, and the foresail was half set. As the waves began breaking over its gunwhale, 'the mothers, wives, sisters, and female friends of the crew joined in the general rush . . . , crying and screaming in agonies to see the poor fellows in the shrouds.' The ship finally grounded midway between Lyme and Charmouth. The rescue that followed was remarkable. A local pilot was lowered from the cliff and succeeded in rescuing the master. One of the crew then fell from the rigging, only to be saved by a Captain Bennet who after being lowered down the cliff dragged him from the sea. The other two members of the crew were so bruised and exhausted that they had to be cut from the rigging and bodily hauled ashore.

The heavy seas created by the 'Great Gale' continued causing damage even when the worst was over. A week later a Lyme trawler foundered off the Cornish coast. That same day a Dutch galliot was wrecked on the Chesil and all on board perished. The gale brought scant benefit to the locals. Their sole source of revenue did not appear until nearly a month later, when another galliot, the *Fortuna*, was wrecked without loss of life opposite the ruins of the Ferry House and some silver coins were found on the beach.

The Coastguard & Lifeboat Services

Prior to the founding of the Royal National Institution for the Preservation of Lives from Shipwreck (later amended to the Royal National Lifeboat Institution) in 1824, all responsibility for saving life at sea and assisting at wrecks was borne by the Coastguard. It was a task for which the Service was ill-equipped. It had once been part of the Preventive Service, and the bitter battles fought between the revenue officers and smuggling gangs had left a legacy of mistrust and suspicion. Its galleys had no extra buoyancy; many of its recruits were elderly naval officers for whom the Service was a form of sinecure. *Punch* summed up its shortcomings, describing the typical station as a 'castle of idleness where able-bodied men spend their time looking through long-glasses for imaginary smugglers.'

Punch's judgement is perhaps harsh. At Swanage alone the station could boast the award of 18 medals for gallantry prior to the arrival of the *Charlotte Mary* in 1875. The crews of the *Aimable Mere* and the brig *Fortitude* must have thought themselves doomed until they saw the St Alban's Head Coastguard galley battling through the surf in appalling conditions in the winter of 1838/39. The other Dorset stations of the early 19th century had equally impressive records, and the lines of coastguard cottages grouped along the coast remain proof of their importance.

As part of the Naval Reserve, the Dorset Coastguard Service maintained the 74 gun *Blenheim,* built in 1813, at Weymouth. Other responsibilities included the administration of the Wild Birds' Protection Act and the reporting of 'Fishes Royal' – any whales or dolphins washed ashore.

The modern Her Majesty's Coastguard is a far cry from its Victorian counterpart. It is now administered by the Board of Trade, and the Dorset coast is covered by the Falmouth Search & Rescue Region, which runs from Padstow to Selsey Bill. The Portland Coastguard acts as the Marine Rescue Sub-Centre and operates a twenty-four hour service; co-ordinating all 'Search & Rescue' missions, helping small boats in trouble, undertaking cliff rescue work, and acting as a monitoring station for distressed vessels. Only recently, in November 1979, it maintained the vital radio link with the *Aeolian Sky* after its fatal collision off Portland. The other Dorset stations are at Poole, Studland, Swanage, St Alban's Head, Kimmeridge, Lulworth, Portland Bill, Fortuneswell and Fleet. The helicopter rescue service for the length of the Dorset coast is covered by the R.N.A.S. at Lee-on-Solent.

The creation of the Royal National Insitution for the Preservation of Lives from Shipwreck in 1824 could not have been more timely. It was the year of the 'Great Gale', and the need for lifeboats and rescue equipment was a favourite topic for the Dorset press. William Morton Pitt, M.P. for Dorchester, was first Secretary of the Dorset Branch Association, and it was he who was instrumental in the acquisition of twelve Manby mortars which were placed along the coast. The mortar had been adapted for life-saving by Captain Manby as a result of his helplessness when a witness to the destruction of the brig *Snipe* a hundred yards off Yarmouth Beach in 1807 with the loss of sixty-seven lives. Leather thongs linked the shot to the line, taking the strain when the

Weymouth lifeboat, Tony Vandervell, *launched in 1976. The 54 feet Arun Class lifeboat is the most modern in service in Dorset. It has a range of 240 miles and a top speed of 18 knots.*

mortar was fired. By 1850 a portable and more efficient rocket apparatus had been placed at Swanage, St Alban's Head, Kimmeridge, Abbotsbury and Langton.

The first purpose-built Dorset lifeboat was launched at Weymouth in 1805, probably in response to the loss of the *Earl of Abergavenny*. Only a prototype was built, and little is now known about its size. Claims that it could carry 'upwards of a 100 men at a time from a wreck' must surely be fanciful? The fourteen men in the crew were fastened to their seats and the mast could be taken down in a storm. It had buoyancy cases, grapnels and life-lines, as well as a 'room ten feet wide, water tight, with copper ventilators'.

Mortars had been issued to the Coastguard at Bridport and Portland in 1815, and there is some scant evidence to suggest that the Shipwreck Association then maintained a lifeboat at Portland, probably a converted lerret. Ten years later a Captain Spencer of the Lyme Regis Coastguard adapted a local boat for life-saving by fitting airtight cases under the thwarts. It was not a success. When first tested it capsized, nearly drowning those on board, and shortly afterwards the copper cases were removed and sold.

In 1826 the Institution provided Dorset with its first official lifeboats. The two 20 feet, six-oared boats, built by Plenty of Newbury, were stationed at Portland and Studland. The Portland boat could be launched either side of the Chesil, but it proved unpopular with the Islanders and was never used to save life. It was sold in 1851, fetching £2 'less 3d for a postal order.' The Studland boat was intended to safeguard the entrance to Poole Harbour, but it too fell into disrepair and had to be sold – without a rescue to its credit. The failure to make use of the two boats remains inexplicable. Wrecks continued to occur, the death toll lengthened. Yet nearly thirty years elapsed before the county was given the lifeboats it so urgently needed.

In 1853 those needs were finally met when a 27 feet eight-oared self-righting lifeboat was placed at Lyme Regis. Within months it had proved its worth, succesfully taking off the crew of the *Jeune Rose* despite capsizing whilst alongside. Twelve years later the *Manley Wood* was wheeled into its house at North Haven Point and Poole could celebrate the arrival of its first lifeboat. From then on progress was swift. By 1875 stations had been opened at Swanage, Chapman's Pool, Kimmeridge and Weymouth. In 1897 Poole took delivery of the *City Masonic Club*, the county's first lifeboat to be equipped with sails. The first motor lifeboat stationed in Dorset was the *Samuel Oakes*, placed at Weymouth in 1924. Some stations have not survived. Those at Kimmeridge and Chapman's Pool had closed by the end of the 19th century due to lack of demand, and the Lyme Regis station was closed between 1932 and 1967, when it was reopened and supplied with an Inshore Rescue Boat.

Lighthouses & Lightships

The earliest Dorset lighthouses illuminate legend rather than fact. For it is only legend that mentions the beacons lit during the middle ages at the chapels on St Adhelm's Head and St Catharine's Hill, Abbotsbury, to warn passing mariners of the dangers ahead. According to one medieval chronicler, St Adhelm's Chapel owes its existence to the deaths of a newly-wed husband and wife who perished in the Race off the headland. In memory of his loss, the girl's father ordered the construction of the chantry chapel so that a priest could pray for the souls of the drowned and a cresset could be lit in bad weather.

By the end of the 17th century the motives for showing lights were no longer so charitable. When in 1699 a London speculator called Sir John Coryton applied for a patent to build a lighthouse on Portland, it was with the intention of levying a toll on all shipping that rounded the Bill. A year later, a Weymouth privateer acting on behalf of the corporation filed a second application to Trinity House, who in turn refused both, on the grounds that no lighthouse was necessary. The number of shipwrecks continued to increase, and in 1716, suspicious that so lucrative a source of revenue was in danger of falling into private hands, Trinity House reversed its own decision, first obtaining a patent then posting tenders for the construction of two lighthouses on Portland Bill.

The upper and lower lighthouses were positioned on the west side of Portland so as to provide a mark for the channel between the Race and the Shambles. They were coal-fired, lit irregularly, and useless in fog. Each acquired its own character; the upper light was erratic, its cousin took time to brighten and often went out in high winds. Despite their defects, Trinity House was soon enjoying an annual £400 income from its investment, made up from the 1d a ton paid by every English vessel that took advantage of the lights, and the 2d from foreign shipping.

The old Upper Lighthouse, Portland, now a Bird Observatory.

In 1788 the upper light was converted to oil and fitted with two rows of Argand lamps – the 14 lamps with their polished metal reflectors were the first to be installed in any English lighthouse. A year later the lower light was replaced. Its 63 feet high successor was built by William Johns of Weymouth on a new site slightly to the east. It was oil-fired, had six lamps and a twenty-two inch lens.

Above the doorway an inscription read:

For the direction and comfort of Navigators;
for the benefit and security of commerce;
and for a lasting memorial of British Hospitality
to all Nations;
this Lighthouse was erected by the ancient
Corporation of Trinity House of
Deptford Strond in 1789
Distance from the cliff 1608 feet.

The change of light does not appear to have led to any significant reduction in the number of Portland shipwrecks in the years that followed: indeed, the disaster that befell Admiral Christian's squadron took place only six years after the rebuilding.

By 1833 the two lighthouses on Portland were producing a combined revenue of £2,300, a considerable sum, and certain proof of the numbers of ships rounding the Bill. New lights were fitted in 1869, and in 1906 they were finally made redundant by the construction of the existing lighthouse on the Bill, a single tower showing both upper and lower lights with a range of 18 miles.

Dorset's only other lighthouse stands on Anvil Point. It was built in 1881, has a range of 18.5 miles, and until modernization in 1959 its light was still turned by clockwork.

The Shambles Lightship was placed at the eastern end of the Shambles in September 1859. In 1969 Trinity House withdrew it from service, replacing it with a navigational buoy.

A Chronological List of Dorset Wrecks

Poole to St Alban's Head

877: destruction of Viking fleet in Swanage Bay (see text).

1306: Bordeaux vessel wrecked 'under Corfe'. 2 dogs and most of the crew survived, but their ship looted and destroyed.

1425: Spanish ship wrecked off Swanage with cargo of wine.

1588: *San Salvador*, capsized in Studland Bay (see text).

1759 March: Poole to Ower passage boat stranded near Furzey Island (see text).

1780: *Fanny*, trading schooner, sank off Peveril Point with cargo of lead ingots.

1786 January 6th: *Halsewell* wrecked under Seacombe Cliffs (see text). March: unknown sloop wrecked near Brownsea Island, all on board lost.

1788 March: *Fame* wrecked on the Hook Sands when bound for Newfoundland and 'got ashore going out of the (Poole) Harbour and bulged.' December: *Rachael*, sloop, ran aground on Hook Sands with some chance of salvage. *Nautilous*, ran ashore on Hook Sands when bound for Bilbao, 'hope will get off next springs by lightening.'

1790 February: *Providence*, inward bound from Liverpool with coal and wrecked on Hook Sands, 'feared will be lost.'

1791 January 18th: *Juno*, bound for London from Lisbon with wine and fruit when ran aground near Harbour entrance. 200 chests of fruit removed by waggon before the planking opened up. February: *Neptune*, bound for London from Swanage with a cargo of stone when it ran aground near Poole and shared the same fate as the *Juno*.

1793 January: *Fanny*, lost 'off Purbeck' when bound for London, crew saved.

1799 February: West Indiaman *Bee* wrecked near Poole but cargo saved (see text). *Eagle*, 50 ton cutter/gunboat 'drove ashore in a violent gale of wind, in Studland Bay.'

1802 July: *Betsey*, bound for Arundel with stone when foundered in Studland Bay, captain and 2 men drowned.

1806 October 2nd: Wareham & Poole passage boat ran aground off Swineham Point (see text).

1810 November 10th: *Dove*, of Southampton, total loss in Studland Bay, all on board drowned.

1813 August: *William & Mary*, sloop, sank in Poole Harbour near the Oyster Bank.

1823 October 12th: *Industrious*, timber laden sloop wrecked on Hook Sands, 2 men saved. November 2nd: *Globe*, lost on Peveril Ledge with cargo of coal. January 14th: *Mary*, smuggling boat, foundered off Christchurch at night, 80 casks of brandy recovered when the coastguard heard the cries of those on board.

1824 March 8th: *Carl Johnn*, brig, wrecked at White Pits, Poole, with cargo of salt and wine, 9 man crew saved. December (or January 1825): *Lark*, small Christchurch vessel, 2 men saved by the coastguard when it was wrecked off 'Flag Head, Branksea Island.'

1837 November: *Sisters*, 101 ton Exeter schooner capsized off Peveril Ledge when running for shelter in Swanage Bay with a cargo of coal. 7 men drowned, 1 saved.

1838: *Aimable Mere*, wrecked off St Alban's Head (see text).

1839 February: *Fortitude*, wrecked off St Alban's Head, 12 man crew rescued by St Alban's Head Coastguard. April: *Jean-Marie*, French brig, wrecked off Swanage, crew of 8 saved by Coastguard. August 7th: *Britannia*, sloop, lost off Purbeck with all on board. December: *Wemyss*, stranded at St Alban's Head.

1847: December 9th: *Robert*, American, drifted on to St Alban's Head whilst on fire.

1848 February 3rd: *Queen*, Lyme built 90 ton sloop wrecked near Poole.

1852 December 27th: *Wiliam Glen Anderson* wrecked off Boscombe in a southerly gale (see text).

1860 April: *Ruby*, brigantine, lost on the Hook Sands.

1864 October 19th: *Union*, wrecked on St Alban's Head.

1865 August: *Twin Brothers*, foundered in Swanage Bay. November 21st: *Virginie*, French lugger, ran on to the rocks near St Alban's Head.

1866 February 11th: *Pallas*, wrecked in Studland Bay. Marked the first launch of Poole's first life-

The Dutch steamer Dorothea *aground on the Chesil near Abbotsbury in February 1914.*

boat, the *Manley Wood*, which was towed out to sea by the wooden paddle tug, *Royal Albert*.

1868 December 15th: two French luggers, the *Augustine* and *Jeune Erneste*, ran aground on the Hook Sands (see text).

1875 January 23rd: *Wild Wave*, brigantine, wrecked on Peveril Ledges during a gale, the crew rescued at dawn by the Coastguard. The loss of *Wild Wave* led to the establishment of Swanage lifeboat station and the arrival of its first lifeboat, the *Charlotte Mary*, in September 1875.

1879 January 7th: *Effort*, Portsmouth ketch, ran ashore off South Haven Point. Crew of 2 taken off by Swanage lifeboat. January 24th: destruction of *Anne Margretha* on Ballard Point (see text).

1881 March 23rd: *Clyde*, lost on Hook Sands.

1882 April 29th: *Alexandrovna*, driven on to rocks to the west of the lighthouse on Anvil Point (see Introduction). June 1st: *Otto*, Swedish brigantine, ran aground on the Milkmaid Shoal with cargo of timber. Crew of 9 taken off by *Boy's Own No. 2*, Poole's second lifeboat.

1883 February 9th: *Moth*, ketch, wrecked 2 miles off Old Harry Rock. September 24th: *Aeolus*, 74 ton schooner, abandoned off Old Harry.

1886 December 26th: *Forest Queen*, brigantine laden with phosphates ran aground off Anvil Point in a gale. Crew of 6 drowned trying to row ashore.

1888 July 24th: *Blanche*, yacht, foundered entering Poole Harbour.

1889 March 7th: *William Maskill*, schooner, inward bound for Southampton from Jersey with coal tar and grease, wrecked on Old Harry Ledge.

circa 1890: *Lord John Russell*, wrecked off Studland with a cargo of Purbeck stone.

1891 November 11th: *Solertia*, foundered in Studland Bay during a gale with cargo of Russian timber for Poole. *Boy's Own No. 2* launched at 4.30 a.m., and after five hours struggling to draw alongside succeeded in taking of crew of 8 and a custom's officer.

1893 December 12th: *Courier*, sank in Poole Harbour during a storm.

1895 January 1st: *Brilliant*, Norwegian barque with cargo of timber foundered on the Hook Sands in snow blizzard and Force 10 winds. Crew of 10 rescued by *Boy's Own No. 2* after Swanage's new lifeboat, *William Erle*, had broached in heavy seas and its coxswain, William Brown, had been drowned.

1898 November 23rd: 3-masted schooner bound for Poole with coal ran ashore in Studland Bay, crew of 6 rescued. The Norwegian 3-masted schooner *Frier* was driven on to the beach at Flag Head Chine on the following day (see text). December 27th: the brig *Marie Therese* lost off Bournemouth.

1900 February: the brigantine *Netto* wrecked on Peveril Ledge.

1906 November 23rd: *Montanes*, steamship, ran aground on St Alban's Head and was soon destroyed.

1908 October 21st: *Conquest*, ketch, driven on to the Milkmaid Shoal after a tow had parted. Originally bound for Cardiff from Poole with a cargo of wheat when worsening weather had forced it to turn back and accept a tow. Crew of 4 rescued.

1910: *Leander*, drifted on to the Hook Sands with bows almost touching Canford Cliffs (see text).

1914 April 22nd: *Envermeu*, steam-coaster, wrecked on the rocks off St Alban's Head in thick fog.

1915 November 13th: King *Heron*, wrecked off Old Harry Ledge, crew of 10 taken off by Poole lifeboat (see text).

1916 October 22nd: *Fame*, wrecked on the Hook Sands (see text). November 5th: *Rose Mysterieuse*, ketch, foundered near Poole. December 7th: *Conch*, lost off Anvil Point.

1917 April 22nd: *Motor Launch 431*, destroyed by fire in Poole Harbour. May 22nd: *Milo*, 1,475 ton steamer, foundered 10 miles south of St Alban's Head.

1919 January 9th: *Zwaluw*, driven ashore in Studland Bay after dragging its anchors in a storm, crew of 9 taken off by Poole lifeboat, *Harmar*. The night of the 8th and 9th proved busy for the *Harmar*, for it also had to take off the 28 man crew of the German submarine *U.143*, outward bound for Japan under the war reparations scheme when it ran aground seeking shelter.

1921 October 8th: *Free Will*, grounded on Peveril Ledges in fog.

1924 November 27th: *Harley*, steamship, foundered off Anvil Point. 18 men drowned, 2 saved.

1927 April 9th: *Kelloch*, lost off Peveril Point with coal for Poole.

1928 May 4th: *Ioannis Fafalios*, Greek steamer sank after collision with Royal Fleet Auxiliary *Bacchus* in fog 20 miles south of St Alban's Head.

1933 December 5th: *Glencora*, small yacht wrecked on the Training Bank, crew of 2 saved.

1939: *Lady of Avenal*, schooner, sank in Holes Bay.

1940 June 23rd: *Leny*, Dutch motor vessel, sank off Handfast Point.

1942 December 21st: *Chausser 5*, free French gunboat, capsized when escorting British submarine in heavy seas. 4 rescued by submarine, 3 saved from upturned hull by Swanage lifeboat in almost impossible conditions; 16 drowned.

1945 Februry 6th: *Everleigh*, steamer, sank off Anvil Point.

1946 April 21st: *Skylark*, Bournemouth pleasure boat sprang a leak off Alum Chine with 70 passengers on board, 1 crew member drowned. December 8th: *Security*, tug, capsized and sank off Anvil Point.

1955 December 12th: *Sandheap*, barge, wrecked on the Milkmaid Shoal when a tow parted.

1975 April 24th: *Elizabeth Robertson*, 60 feet fishing boat, gutted by fire 7 miles south of St Alban's Head. 2 man crew lifted off by helicopter.

1979 November 3rd: *Aeolian Sky*, 16,000 ton Greek steamer collided with *Anna Knuepell*, West German coaster, in the early morning off Portland. The *Aeolian Sky* was taken in tow, but it sank off Anvil Point on the 4th when it began shipping water and entry into Portsmouth proved impossible. The crew was taken off by helicopter. Mystery still surrounds its loss, for its was carrying £1,200,000 of Seychelles rupees which proved to have vanished when divers went down to the wreck.

St Alban's Head to Weymouth

1371: *Welfare*, driven ashore in Kimmeridge Bay and deliberately plundered (see text).

1680 September 15th: *Agreement*, pink, sank in Weymouth Harbour (see text).

1681 April 28th: *Success*, wrecked near Weymouth with cargo of wine.

1697 December 24th: *Dove*, wrecked at Lulworth with cargo of wine.

1699 April: a ship laden with Spanish wines wrecked near Weymouth.

1701 January 20th: a ship lost in Weymouth Bay, all on board drowned, 15 tons of logwood washed ashore at Weymouth. February: *La Notre Dame de Montaigne*, stranded near Weymouth.

1702: *Katherine*, wrecked near Weymouth. Revenue smack *Weymouth* wrecked in the same storm (see text).

1707 November: *Joanah*, outward bound from Lisbon, wrecked near Weymouth and only 1 man saved (see text).

1734: Records mention 'a small wrecke having been thrown upon' a farm at West Lulworth.

1742 January 12th: letter by the Collector at Weymouth Custom's House mentions the discovery of a vessel on the shore at Osmington (see Introduction).

1745 October 23rd: unidentified wreck at Hamburrow Farm, Lulworth. The Dorset County Records Office contains an account of what was found, listing the masts, sails, blocks and 'small cordage of small value'.

1758 February 12th: unnamed sloop bound from Weymouth to Portsmouth with a cargo of malt lost off Lulworth, all on board drowned.

1770 April 28th: custom's boat lost off Weymouth whilst searching for smugglers, 8 drowned (see text).

1772 November 10th: *Suky*, brig, capsized in St

Alban's Race and only one survivor. Its cargo of wine consumed by the local villagers.

1774 October 3rd: *Neptune*, Swedish, laden with sugar and coffee, foundered off Weymouth and 8 men drowned.

1791 January 18th: *Lottery*, sloop, driven ashore near Weymouth.

1795 November 18th: *Pitt*, wrecked off Purbeck in the same storm that destroyed 6 ships of Admiral Christian's fleet on the Chesil.

1802 July 26th: *Norwich*, laden with coal from Sunderland when it struck the anchor of another ship in Weymouth harbour and sank.

1813 April 17th: *St Johannes*, from Seville for London with cargo of fruit when it foundered off the Purbeck coast.

1825 December 14th: *Vigilant*, wrecked at Lulworth, 1 man saved by coastguards.

1826 September 29th: *John Rickard*, struck Kimmeridge Ledges in fog with cargo of rum, sugar, cocoa and cotton.

1827 January: *Jon*, French smack lost off Weymouth with no survivors.

circa 1836: *Hound*, revenue cutter, wrecked off Weymouth race ground (see text).

1838: *Joseph Desire*, wrecked at Kimmeridge, 8 man crew rescued by coastguards. The storm of November 28th-30th: *Marie Louise*, French brig, wrecked at Bowleaze. 6 out of 7 rescued. Coastguard John Mantle awarded gold medal by Royal Humane Society for saving 2 boys. One French ship driven ashore at West Lulworth, another at Kimmeridge.

1855 January 18th: *Ino*, brig, wrecked on Weymouth Beach.

1856 September: *Caernavon Castle*, sloop, wrecked on Cuttle Ledge, Kimmeridge, crew of 4 saved by coastguards.

1861 January 20th: *Hardy*, 374 ton barque wrecked on Kimmeridge Ledges (see text). February 14th: *Dorothy*, coastal coal schooner, wrecked close to *Hardy*.

1866 January: *Georgina*, 400 ton French barque driven ashore at Chapman's Pool (see text).

1868 September 25th: *Liberty*, Portsmouth schooner, slipped off the reef at Broad Bench and sank with the loss of all on board (see text).

1872 December 9th: *Stralsund*, Norwegian square-rigger wrecked on the east side of Kimmeridge Bay (see text).

1874 November: *Foam*, wrecked on Weymouth Beach.

1877 August 18th: *Commodore*, wrecked on Encombe Ledge (see text).

1878 December 2nd: *Gipsy Queen*, 3 masted schooner, inward bound for Newcastle from the West Indies with guano, wrecked on Kimmeridge Ledges.

1879 February 7th: *Essay*, smack, wrecked at Weymouth. November 24th: *Catherine McIver*, schooner, wrecked on Encombe Ledge with cargo of china clay.

1880 November 19th: *Arklow*, 500 ton steamer bound for Southampton, wrecked on Kimmeridge Ledges in fog.

1881 November 27th: *Jeanne Elise*, French schooner, wrecked near Osmington. December 7th: *Marie Joseph*, French schooner, wrecked near Preston Coastguard Station.

1883 Christmas Day: *South of Ireland*, Great Western Railway steamer, wrecked on the rocks in Worbarrow Bay.

1886 March 21st: *Ceres*, Poole cutter with cargo of Cornish barley, ran ashore in fog at Broad Bench. 1 man drowned, 3 rescued. May 15th: *Palala*, 1,408 ton steamer, wrecked on Kimmeridge Ledges with no loss of life – lengthy salvage operations followed.

1887 November 1st: *Maren*, Danish brigantine, wrecked in Weymouth Bay, 7 saved. The Spanish steamer *Mayo* ran aground on the west side of St Alban's Head on the same day.

1891 March 9th: *Bildene*, wrecked near Preston Coastguard Station.

1898 December 31st: *Ada*, ketch, wrecked in Kimmeridge Bay in southerly gale when in ballast between Southampton and Cherbourg.

1899 February 13th: *Stuart*, steamship, broke adrift in a gale and went aground between Preston and Osmington.

1900 November 10th: *Hildegarde*, steamer with Spanish iron ore bound for Newcastle, wrecked on Freshwater Ledges.

1909 November 14th: *Morning Star*, ketch, stranded on Kimmeridge Ledges.

1914 December 11th: *Ardente*, French schooner, grounded in Weymouth Bay. Crew of 5 rescued by Weymouth lifeboat *Friern Watch*.

1915 January 1st: *Otto*, Russian brig, and the Dutch ketch *Zwaatje Cornelia*, driven ashore near Preston.

1920 January 9th: 5,500 ton steamer *Treveal* wrecked on Kimmeridge Ledges with the loss of 36 lives (see text).

1922 March 24th: *Glenmore*, steamer, sank after striking the wreck of the *Treveal*.

1939 October 20th: *Turkie*, Greek steamer, wrecked at Houns Tout Cliff near Chapman's Pool. Crew of 26 saved by Swanage lifeboat which remained on duty for 74 hours.

1943 January: *Bloodhound*, M.T.B., wrecked near Weymouth.

1945 December 10th: *T.A. Johnston*, American 'Liberty' ship, grounded at Egmont Point (see text).

1948 June 6th: *Mite*, wrecked in Ringstead Bay.

The 5,500 ton Patroclus, *laden with wool and bananas, after striking Blacknor Point in September 1907. It took 4 tugs, a salvage vessel and 11 steam pumps to finally refloat it.*

1966 September 4th: *Faem*, yacht, grounded near Kimmeridge.
1967 May 13th: *Patricia Two*, yacht, sank off Kimmeridge.
1974 September 4th: *Elver*, yacht, wrecked in Lulworth Cove.
1976 October 14th: *Scandia*, 33 feet yacht washed on to Weymouth Beach.
1979 December 18th: *Caroline of Leigh*, 36 feet yacht, sank 3 miles off Lulworth with the loss of 4 lives.

The Isle of Portland

1305: Spanish ship wrecked and looted on Portland (see text).
1311: *Sainte Goymelote*, boarded by Portlanders and deliberately wrecked (see text).
1667: *HMS Pembroke*, 28 guns, sunk off Portland after collision with the *Fairfax*.
1676: A hoy of London 'cast away' on Portland Beach.
1681 December 14th: *Angel Guardian*, wrecked off Portland Beach with cargo of oranges.
1685 November 1st: *Peter*, wrecked on Portland Beach with cargo of French wine.
1701 December: French ship bound for Amsterdam stranded near Portland with a cargo of wine, soap and capers.
1706 August: ship carrying tin wrecked off Portland with no survivors. The Islanders later dredged up 150 blocks of tin.
1717 February: French vessel looted after being wrecked on Portland Beach (see text).
1762 January: *HMS Cormorant*, 32 guns, ran aground on the Shambles. Cornish vessel foundered near Portland, the Islanders later seizing its cargo of brandy from the revenue officers (see text).
1776 November: Dutch ketch lost in the Race. 2 casks of turpentine later picked up by 'servants of the Weld family.'
1778 October: *La Bien-Aime*, sloop, wrecked on Portland and cargo of brandy later stolen from locked building by cutting through the thatch (see text).
1780: A Cowes vessel driven by a storm into Cave Hole Cavern, Portland Bill.
1793 March 18th: 90 ton French brigantine with a cargo of salt, a prize of the frigate *HMS Crescent*, wrecked near Portland Castle with no loss of life.
1796 May 30th: *Peggy*, 180 tons, wrecked on Portland with a cargo of bark, cotton and hides. 8 drowned, 3 saved.

1797: *Amazon*, part of the wreckage washed up on Portland.

1798: *Duchess of York:* lost with all hands near the Bill.

1805 February 5th: *Earl of Abergavenny*, East Indiaman, wrecked in Weymouth Bay with the loss of 234 lives after striking the Shambles (see text).

1806 November: a brig wrecked on Portland Beach, cargo and crew both lost. French chasse-marée driven ashore on Portland with cargo of wheat and beans. 2 drowned, 2 saved.

1819 January 11th: *William Kedger*, wrecked on Portland Beach with cargo of oranges.

1820 October 17th: *Pollux*, brig, bound for London from Cork, wrecked on the Beach with cargo of wheat, flour, butter and beef. 1 drowned.

1821 April 4th: *Spritly*, wrecked on Portland with 5 Islanders on board, all drowned. Another vessel, the *Taberan*, was wrecked on the same day.

1826 September 6th: *Francis Feeling*, packet, run down and sunk by a Swedish brig off Portland. 16 drowned (see text).

1827 March: *Charles*, Scarborough brig wrecked off Portland.

1827 December: *City of Limerick*, stranded in 'Bagg's Hole . . . with no chance of getting off' after being driven from Portland Roads in a storm.

1830 February 23rd: *Meteor*, packet paddle-steamer, wrecked in Church Ope Cove with no casualties. Later looted (see text).

1832 December 24th: unnamed sloop foundered off Portland after springing a leak. 3 drowned, 1 saved.

1838 December 7th: *Herberts Anker*, Norwegian brig, wrecked on Portland Beach.

1839 January 19th: *Commodore*, schooner, foundered off Portland. Crew saved.

1840 October 26th: *Delight*, schooner, foundered off Portland. Crew saved.

1841 November 30th: *Amyntas* Exeter brig, driven ashore on Portland Beach. 2 men saved by local coastguards. Its loss led to the creation of the Portland Marine Humane Society.

1857 March 8th: *Hope*, Lyme smack, foundered in the Race. Crew of 3 rescued by French fishing smack *Victorie Desirée* whose master was later awarded the Institution's silver medal. March 24th: *Hebrides*, barque, wrecked on Portland.

1860 February: *Albert*, schooner, wrecked on Portland Breakwater – as was the Norwegian barque *Irene* on December 12th, and the Plymouth schooner *Norval* on December 30th.

1865: November 22nd: *Emmanuel*, French brig, wrecked in Chesil Cove.

1866 July 10th: collision of the *Amazon* and *Osprey* off Portland. The *Osprey* sank instantly with the loss of 10 lives. The *Amazon* picked up the 22 survivors, but was later abandoned and sank (see text).

1867 December 31st: *Judy*, 150 ton coal schooner, wrecked in a south-westerly gale on Godner Ledge near the Bill.

1868 January 21st: *Junior*, Cornish schooner bound for Poole with cargo of clay, foundered when a change of wind swept it into the Race. January 28th: *Bank*, 500 ton barque carrying pickled onions, coal, coke and fire bricks, wrecked in Broad Hope Cave and later sold for 8/-: barrels of pickled onions later washed up on the beach found their way into the Islanders diet.

1869 February 2nd: *Henry & Dora*, 119 ton brigantine, wrecked after striking the Breakwater. September 12th: *Salathiel*, wrecked on the Breakwater. November 1st: *Jacoba Catherina*, Dutch schooner, sank midway between the Shambles and Breakwater.

1872 March: *Surprise*, of Bridport, wrecked in light winds in the Race.

1873 February 25th: collision between the 550 ton Genoese barque *No* and the French ship *Gasland* 13 miles s.w. of Portland. November 7th: *Caaermano de Camarinas*, Spanish brig, wrecked in Balaclava Bay.

1874 November 29th: *Sultan*, 50 ton smack, sank after drifting on to the Breakwater in a gale.

1875 January 24th: *Marie Reine*, 600 ton coal-laden barque wrecked in Chesil Cove. 4 drowned.

1876 January 11th: collision of the *Annie Edwin* and the Norwegian brig *Nordkap* 8 miles off Portland. March 12th: *Athlete*, schooner, sank in gale. 7 out of 8 drowned. The ship's boy, who was picked up alive, was on his first voyage and not certain of the name of the ship. December 5th: unnamed schooner seen to founder off Portland. 5 drowned. December 13th: *Anemone*, brigantine, sank after collision with 141 ton Norwegian barque *Hannah Parr* in Lyme Bay.

1877 September 11th: collision off Portland of the *Avalanche* and *Forest* with the loss of 108 lives (see text).

1878 October 10th: *British Seaman*, 176 ton coal schooner sank after collision with the Greek vessel *Antipi*.

1879 October 20th: *Thomas & Mary*, sank off Sandsfoot Castle (see Introduction).

1881 December 22nd: *Pater*, Austrian barque, wrecked at Saltpool.

1882 September 6th: Dutch galliot lost after collision with Liverpool barque *Comadre*.

1883 June 22nd: collision of the *Waitara* and *Hurunui* off Portland with the loss of 26 lives (see text). August 8th: *Sapphire*, coal schooner, wrecked in Chesil Cove.

1886 August 27th: *Bournemouth*, excursion paddle-steamer, wrecked beneath the higher lighthouse on the Bill (see text). October 14/15th: *Zamia*, 500 tons, towed into Portland after capsizing with the loss of all on board.

1887 October 30th: *Laureate*, cutter, wrecked on Breakwater. 10 drowned.

1888 August 14th: *Lady Sondes*, ketch, lost off Portland.

1890 April 21st: *Ehen*, drifted on shore in Mutton Cove when bound for Bremen from Bordeaux with rice and pickle.

1891 January 2nd: *Thames*, steamer, wrecked in Chesil Cove. March 10th: *Neptune*, steamer, wrecked off Portland. November 11th: *Amphitrite*, coal hulk, wrecked on the Breakwater.

1894 March 5th: *Lord Duflus*, schooner, wrecked on the Bill. August 26th: *Gertrude*, steamship, stranded on Blacknor Point.

1896 July: *Siren*, sank after being rammed by HMS *Landrail*.

1899 August 5th: *Netley Abbey*, sank after collision with unidentified warship 8 miles from Shambles light-vessel.

The barque Ehen, *wrecked after grounding in Mutton Cove, Portland in April 1890 with its cargo of rice and pickles.*

1900 December 29th: *Enecuri*, Spanish steamer, wrecked after striking the Breakwater. Captain drowned returning to his ship, crew of 26 saved.

1903 July 22nd: *Verbena*, ketch, wrecked near Blacknor Point. September 10th: *Missions to Seamen*, cutter, sank off Portland in a gale.

1905: *Devoran*, schooner, possibly rammed by unidentified destroyer.

1906 February 6th: *Star of Peace*, lost of the Bill.

1910 January 15th: *Spirit*, pilot boat, sank after collision with Danish steamer *St Jan*. July 18th: *Haytian*, coal hulk, rammed and sunk in the Harbour (see text). October 31st: *Recca Nova*, formerly the Cosens steamer *Brodick Castle*, sunk off Portland whilst in tow to Argentina as a converted cattle barge.

1912 March 25th: *Myrtledene*, 2,500 steamer, wrecked in Mutton Cove. December 10th: *Derna*, Italian steamer, sank after colliding with battleship *HMS Centurion* 30 miles west of the Bill.

1913 February 2nd: *Turenne*, French trawler, lost at Clay Hope.

1914 July 30th: *Lucinda*, schooner, gutted by fire 14 miles off Portland. September 17th: *Fisgaro III*, naval training ship, capsized whilst being towed with the loss of 21 lives. November 4th:

The 2,500 ton iron-ore carrying steamer Myrtledene *in Mutton Cove in March 1912: The 26 people on board were taken off by the Coastguard but the ship was completely wrecked.*

HMS Hood, 14,000 ton battleship, placed in southern entrance to Portland Harbour and deliberately sunk to block the entrance.

1917 December 22nd: *Clan Cameron*, steamer, sank 22 miles off Portland.

1918 January 4th: *Golden Sunset*, naval trawler, sank near Shambles Lightship after collision. January 28th: *Hazard*, torpedo gunboat, sank off the Bill after collision. April 4th: *HMS Bittern*, destroyer, sank off the Bill after collision.

1920 January 16th: *James Fennell*, trawler, wrecked on Blacknor Point.

1922 December 20th: *Scandinavia*, sank after striking the Breakwater (see text).

1923 February 22nd: *Phoenix*, ketch, sank after striking the Breakwater. April: *Freewill*, salvage vessel, sank whilst working on the *Scandinavia* (see text).

1924 January 10th: *L-24*, submarine, lost after collision west of the Bill (see text).

1926 December 2nd: *Eugene Schneider*, French barque, sank after collision with steamer *Burutu* off Portland.

1927 December 28th: *Lily*, pilot boat, sank in the Harbour with the loss of 2 lives.

1930 January 12th: *Forester*, 78 ton coaster, sank in the Harbour. The crew of 6 and a stowaway scrambled on to the Breakwater. September 20th: *Madelaine Tristan*, schooner, wrecked in Chesil Cove. *Inisinver*, steamer, sank off the Bill on an unknown date.

1931 January 13th: *Crown of Denmark*, wrecked on the Breakwater.

1932 January 26th: *M2*, submarine, lost 3 miles west of the Bill (see text). *Sodern*, Swedish steamer, wrecked off Portland at an unkown date.

1935 September 16th: *Countess of Erne*, paddle-steamer converted to coal-hulk, sank in the Harbour.

1943 December 24/25th: *Lily*, naval auxiliary, sank off Portland after collision.

1945 September 19th: *Minerve*, French submarine, wrecked at the Bill after a tow parted.

1946 January 7th: *Opha*, 150 tons, wrecked off the Bill. December 11th: *Marguerita*, trawler, wrecked on the Bill with the loss of 7 lives.

The French trawler Turenne *before being wrecked at Clay Hope, Portland, in 1913.*

The Madelaine Tristan *on the Chesil in 1930. The French grain schooner was later sold for £1, but only its masts were removed and the wreck was a familiar sight until its eventual destruction by the sea.*

1948 October 18th: loss of 'Liberty' boat from *HMS Illustrious* in the Harbour. 29 drowned, 21 survivors (see text).

1949 June 4th: *Reliance*, ketch, lodged in cave to the east of the Bill. Ann Davison, whose husband was drowned, later described the tragedy in a book, *Last Voyage*.

1951 September 8th: *Lendor*, 15 ton yacht, wrecked on the Bill.

1955 June 16th: *Sidon*, submarine, sank in the Harbour after an explosion. 13 men drowned. The *Sidon* was later raised, but in 1957 it was deliberately sunk off Portland for ASDIC training (see text).

1961 June 24th: *Evertsen*, steamship, sank off the Bill after a collision.

1968 August 16th: *Naiad*, yacht, wrecked off Portland.

1974 September 7th: *Greta C*, freighter, sank off Portland.

The Chesil Beach

1600 Christmas Day: *Isobel*, privateer, and 20 other ships reputedly wrecked in the same storm (see Introduction).

1629 January: Spanish ship wrecked off Burton Bradstock and looted.

1641 December: *Golden Grape*, wrecked near Wyke Regis when bound for Dover from Cadiz (see text).

1706 January: *Golden Fleece*, lost on the Chesil.

1716 January: *Jesus Maria Joseph*, wrecked on the Chesil. Customs men failed to recover the cargo because looters 'Beat, Hounded and Resisted us in the Salvidge.'

1742 February: unknown ship foundered off the Beach. The customs men 'caused a thorough Rummage' but found nothing of value.

1749 January 16th: *Hope*, Dutch East Indiaman, wrecked and looted opposite Fleet (see text).

1754 November 9th: *Charming Molly*, lost off Wyke. 2 men buried on the beach.

1758: ship carrying timber stranded near West Bexington.

circa 1760: *Squirrel*, wrecked with cargo of tobacco off Abbotsbury.

1762 January 12th: *Zenobie*, French privateer, wrecked in Chesil Cove (see text).

1767 March 7th: *Peggy*, wrecked off Chesil (see text under Portland).

1773 February: *Johannes*, wrecked and looted on Chesil.

1774 September 22nd: Dutch ship lost on the Beach. 8 drowned, 3 saved.

1780 April 17th: *Blandford*, 50 ton sloop carrying copper and tin, wrecked on Fleet Bank.

1781 January 30th: *Theresa*, 110 ton Flemish brigantine laden with coal, wrecked off Bexington. February 13th: *Amsterdam*, 220 ton Swedish brigantine, wrecked off Bexington with cargo of raisins, 'very few of which will be saved owing to the ship's going to pieces as soon as she struck.' 5 drowned.

1795 November 18th: *Aeolus*, *Golden Grove*, *Thomas*, *Piedmont*, *Venus* and *Catherine* all wrecked on the Chesil (see text). The *Hannah* was also wrecked in the same storm.

1797 December 17th: *Marquis of Worcester*, West Indiaman, wrecked near Fleet House returning from St Vincent with cargo of sugar. 23 drowned, 1 saved.

1799 September 22nd: *Concord*, in ballast, lost off Abbotsbury. The *Rodney* and *De trende Sodikende* were wrecked on the Beach in the same storm.

1807 January 9th: *Johanna Elizabeth*, Swedish galliot, wrecked off Abbotsbury with cargo of salt and wines. 2 drowned, 6 saved.

1815 March 27th: *Alexander*, East Indiaman, wrecked opposite Wyke (see text).

1818 March 4th: *Le Mercuria*, 500 ton French vessel, lost near Chesil Cove. 20-30 drowned.

1821 March 18th: *Arthur le Juvenale*, French brig carrying coffee and cotton, wrecked at Langton.

1823 November 10th: *Iris*, Swedish brig, lost on Chesil (see text).

1824 December 19th: *Fortuna*, Dutch galliot carrying tobacco and wine, wrecked opposite the Ferry House.

1831 December 7th: *Atlas*, American brig, wrecked on Chesil. 2 drowned, 9 saved.

1835 October 25th: *Margaret & Ann*, schooner carrying Welsh slate, lost on Chesil in a 'perfect hurricane'. All on board lost, 5 bodies found.

1837 November 24th: *Izstrarne*, Swedish, wrecked off Burton Bradstock. 4 drowned, 3 saved. The ship's steward, Olaff Bjorkholm, is buried in Burton Bradstock and an entry in the Burial Register records the wreck.

1838 November 28th-30th: *Mary Ann*, schooner, lost off Abbotsbury. *Arethusa*, lost off Fleet with no survivors. *Louise*, Swedish barque, thrown unladen on to the Chesil without loss of life. *Dove*, 70 ton local trader, abandoned in West Bay and wrecked on the Chesil. The *Dove* had been captured by the French in 1806 and its master, Peter Bussell, had been imprisoned until 1814. *Columbine*, schooner, lost west of Wyke. *Le Jean Bart*, French smack, first seen off Bridport but wrecked near Burton Bradstock with cargo of hides. 4 drowned, 5 saved by local villagers who hauled them from the wreck to the top of the 200 feet cliff. Other ships were wrecked in the same storm, some on the Chesil, some off-shore.

1840 January 24th: *Saggitario*, Austrian polacco bound for Constantinople with timber, cloth and sùgar, wrecked near Chesil. 13 man crew rescued. It was described at the time as a 'pirate vessel'.
1851 January 17th: *Vriendshap Heike*, Dutch galliot, wrecked near Fleet and later sold on the. Beach.
1852 December 27th: *Nouvelle Loire*, French barque, broke into 2 pieces before striking.
1856 December 9th: *Petronilia*, Belgian barque, wrecked on the Chesil and crew of 4 buried in St George's churchyard.
1857: *Little Belt*, smack, lost on the Chesil.
1866 January 14th: *Ocean Bride*, schooner, wrecked opposite Langton.
1872 November 23rd: *Jane Catherine*, 70 ton schooner carrying shale, wrecked between Wyke and Fleet within 40 yards of the shore. 4 drowned. November 25th: *Royal Adelaide*, iron-built emigrant clipper, wrecked on the Chesil and looted (see text).
1875 January 24th: *Marie Reine*, French barque, lost on the Chesil.
1879 January 7th: *Speedy*, lost opposite Ferry Bridge.
1882 January 5th: *Edwin & Sarah*, ketch, wrecked in Chesil Cove. *Result*, ketch, wrecked on the Chesil in about 1882.
1887 January 18th: *Nor*, 943 ton Norwegian schooner-rigged steamer, wrecked on the Beach in thick fog with cargo of salt.
1888 March 8th: *Lanoma*, 665 ton iron-built barque, wrecked near Fleet with 2,000 bales of Tasmanian wool. 12 drowned, 6 saved. The *Lanoma* was a purpose-built wool clipper and had once completed the Australian run in 63 days.
1889 March 8th: *Vera*, 2,019 Hull steamer, wrecked near Langton exactly a year after the loss of the *Lanoma*. The crew of 24, 3 passengers, and 2 nine-year-old stowaways were rescued by coastguards.
1890 October 31st: *Fannie C*, schooner, beached in Chesil Cove whilst on fire. 10 saved.
1891 October 13th: *Ora et Labora*, Norwegian brig, wrecked near Chesil Cove.
1894 August 26th: *Gertrude*, wrecked on the Chesil.
1897: *Flirt*, wrecked on the Beach near Burton Bradstock.
1903 October 25th: *Emma Maria*, Russian schooner, lost on Chesil with cargo of fire-clay. The Norwegian barque *Patria* was wrecked close to the *Emma Maria* on the following day and its crew taken off using the rocket apparatus.
1914 January 7th: *Cora*, French schooner, lost on the Beach.
1920 January 15th: *Preveza*, Greek steamer, wrecked on the Chesil in thick fog.

The steamship Gertrude *after being stranded in thick fog on Blacknor Point in August 1894.*

The Russian schooner Emma Maria *breaking up on the Chesil in October 1903. The barque* Patria *was wrecked on the same part of the Beach on the following day.*

1944 October 13th: *LC(T) A.2454*, American tank landing craft, wrecked on the Chesil in south-westerly gale. The Weymouth lifeboat, *William & Clara Ryland*, was preparing to take off the crew when the naval authorities ashore ordered it to stand off, lest it also be wrecked. 3 men were saved using rocket apparatus, then the apparatus was swept away and 2 coastguards were drowned.

1963 July 15th: *Bassurelle*, French trawler, wrecked off Langton. 5 saved.

1974 January 25th-29th: *Scaldis*, sank off Chesil with the loss of 3 lives.

Bridport to Lyme Regis

1280: Unnamed wreck at Bridport Creek.

1377 November: 50 ships reputedly lost at Lyme Regis in a series of storms (see text).

1670: A Lyme barque wrecked at Bridport. Two vessels from Lyme also wrecked (see text).

1709 December 25th: *HMS Solebay*, wrecked at Lyme (see text).

1748 July: *Laguiticus de Lille Dieu* lost off Lyme with cargo of wool, all on board saved (see text).

1789 August: *Endeavour*, brig, left Sidmouth for Newcastle to load with coal, wrecked near Bridport, 'the crew were with difficulty saved.'

1812 February 21st: *Fox*, London to Exeter schooner, driven ashore near Bridport and wrecked. *Henrietta*, London smack wrecked near Bridport.

1817 January: *Trois Amis* wrecked near Bridport during gales. *Volante*, *Mary* and *Union* all wrecked at Lyme. Unnamed French chasse-marée wrecked on Charmouth Beach (see text).

1829: *Magnet*, foundered in Lyme Bay. Part of the wreckage washed ashore at Bridport in the following year. July 1st: *Prince William*, Liverpool sloop, misread signal flags during a gale when entering Bridport and wrecked on rocks to the west. Captain washed overboard, crew of 3 saved.

1832 March 1st: *Swallow*, Bridport based, driven ashore near the Harbour.

1836 December: *William & Anne*, wrecked at Lyme (see text).

1846 November 20th: *Colyton Union*, 72 ton coaster wrecked at Lyme, where it had been built in 1826.

1851 mid-January: gale from the south-south-west. Smack lost 5 miles out from Bridport. Remains

The two sections of the Preveza *on the beach in Chesil Cove after it had broken up during a storm in 1920. The boilers remained visible for many years.*

of the *Jessy*, of Plymouth, washed up at Bridport with 2 other small Exeter boats. *Mary Ann*, schooner, wrecked at Lyme just east of the Cobb, crew saved.

1852 December 26th: *Heroine*, wrecked at Lyme (see text). The local boat *Sarah* was wrecked on the following day.

1854 January 7th: *Jeune Rose*, foundered off Lyme (see text).

1860 November 14th: *Elizabeth Ann*, Lyme smack laden with coal wrecked on rocks near the Cobb. 3 man crew taken off by lifeboat.

1865 November: *Black Diamond* wrecked at Bridport (see text).

1867 January 8th: localized south-westerly gale at Lyme led to the loss of the schooners *Ann & Emily*, *Vulcan*, and *Panda*, and the *Spec*, brigantine – all local ships. 3 men rescued by coastguard cutter as it was impossible to launch the lifeboat.

1868 January 24th: *Marie Leocadie*, wrecked at Bridport (see text).

1869 January 22nd: *Demetrius*, ran ashore opposite watch-house at Bridport (see text). December 30th: *Louise et Eugenie*, French brig laden with wheat from Dunkirk, blown off course and wrecked 200 yards west of Bridport Harbour wall, 2 men drowned.

1870 January 16th: *Laura*, 9 man crew saved after the 307 ton vessel had sprung a leak and sunk 20 miles south of Bridport. October 26th: *Kennet*, wrecked at Bridport (see text).

1871 March 15th: *Collingwood*, wrecked near Lyme Regis.

1874 December 12th: *Corsair*, 119 tons, wrecked on Seatown Beach.

1881 October 31st: *Flying Fish*, wrecked near Cobb, Lyme Regis.

1887 August 27th: *King George*, 40 ton trawler laden with limestone from Lyme Regis, went ashore among the Black Rocks to the west of West Bay and sank.

1891 October: two Shoreham smacks driven ashore at West Bay during a gale.

1895 January 18th: *Olive*, holed in calm weather at West Bay and eventually sank (see text).

1903 March 12th: *Albion*, grit carrying schooner wrecked on the beach at West Bay after colliding with the west pier.

1909 November 27th: *Lancelot*, sprit-sail barge

driven ashore near West Bay.

1913 November 4th: *Empress of India*, 14,000 ton battleship deliberately sunk in Lyme Bay whilst being used as a naval target.

1914 December 11th: *Emma & John*, Weymouth fishing smack wrecked on the cliffs to the east of Lyme Regis in southerly gale.

1923 May 3rd: *Alioth*, wrecked on beach to east of West Bay (see text).

1924 January 12th: *Nordead*, French mud-hopper drived ashore at Seatown with no one on board.

1930 January 12th: *Reine des Cieux*, French ketch, seen drifting across Lyme Bay after crew taken off by Torbay lifeboat. Eventually wrecked at Eype, just west of Bridport.

1937 January 31st: *St Michel*, French ketch, wrecked between Charmouth and Lyme.

1969 January 17th: *Karuna*, catamaran, abandoned at sea after collision with tanker and towed into Lyme. Broke its moorings during a gale. Two lifeboatmen drowned when attempting to recover it and the Inshore Rescue Boat capsized.

NOTE: The Index does not include ships wrecked in the 'Great Gale' of 1824, but their names are listed between pages 41 and 43.

Vessels sunk by Enemy Action

Ailsa Craig: steamship, sunk by torpedo in Lyme Bay. 15.4.1918.

Albert C Field: 1,764 ton ammunition ship, sunk off Anvil Point. 18.6.1944.

Alex Van Opstal: 5,900 ton Belgian liner, mined and sunk on the east side of Portland Bill. 15.9.1939.

Algarve: steamship, torpedoed and sunk 15 miles w.s.w. of Portland Bill with the loss of 21 lives. 20.10.1917.

Aparima: 5,704 tons, torpedoed 6 miles off Anvil Point with the loss of 56 lives. 19.11.1917.

Avanti: steamship, torpedoed 4 miles off Anvil Point with the loss of 22 lives. 2.2. 1918.

Bamse: torpedoed 15 miles off Portland Bill. 17.4.1918.

Baron Garioch: torpedoed 5 miles off Anvil Point. 28.10.1917.

Baygitano: 3,073 ton steamship, torpedoed 1½ miles off Lyme Regis with the loss of 3 lives. 18.3.1918.

Binnendijk: Dutch freighter, mined near the Shambles Lightship. 7.10.1939.

Black Hawk: American steamship, torpedoed off Worbarrow, where it later beached on the reef. 29.12.1944.

Blackwood: 1,150 ton frigate, torpedoed off Portland. 15.6.1944.

Boadicea: destroyer, sunk off Portland by aerial torpedo. 13.6.1944.

Borga: steamship, torpedoed 9 miles off Beer Head with the loss of 9 lives. 1.3.1918.

British Inventor: steam tanker, mined 5 miles off St Alban's Head and sank whilst in tow. 13.6.1940.

Broomhill: 1,392 ton collier, sunk by submarine gunfire 9 miles south-west of Portland Bill. 10.5.1917.

L.H. Carl: 1,916 ton steamer, torpedoed in Lyme Bay with the loss of 2 lives. 20.7.1917.

Clan Macvey: 5,815 tons, sunk by torpedo off Anvil Point with the loss of 7 lives. 8.8.1918

Crane: Norwegian steamship, torpedoed off Portland Bill. 9.3.1918.

HMS Delight: 1,375 ton destroyer, bombed and sank off Portland. 26.7.1940.

Elena. R: 5,900 ton Greek steamship, mined off the Shambles. 22.11.1939.

Elmcrest: 4,343 ton steamer, sunk by E-boat 13 miles south of the Bill. 4.7.1940.

Ermenilda: captured by submarine and destroyed 24 miles s.s.w. of Portland. 4.8.1916.

HMS Formidable: 15,000 ton battleship, sunk by torpedo in Lyme Bay with the loss of 551 lives. 1.1.1915.

Fortuna: steam vessel, captured by submarine and destroyed 15 miles s.s.w. of Portland Bill. 3.8.1916.

Foylebank: 5,582 ton anti-aircraft ship, bombed and sunk in Portland Harbour. 4.7.1980. The Victoria Cross was posthumously awarded to Leading Seaman J. Mantle for remaining at the starboard 'pom-pom' and firing back even though mortally wounded. It was the first V.C. awarded to a rating in the war. The *Foylebank*'s bows were raised in 1948, the remainder was salvaged in 1952.

Gibel-Hamam: steamship, torpedoed off Abbotsbury with the loss of 14 lives. 14.9.1918.

Hartburn: torpedoed 10 miles south of Anvil Point with the loss of 3 lives. 15.10.1917.

Hartlepool: steamship, sunk by gunfire in the entrance to Weymouth Harbour. 5.7.1940.

Hazlewood: 3,120 tons, torpedoed 8 miles south-east of Anvil Point with the loss of 32 lives. 18.10.1917.

Hickory: motor vessel, mined off Portland Bill. 22.10.1940.

Himalaya: 4,690 ton coal hulk, sunk by bombing in Portland Harbour. 12.6.1940. When launched in 1853 the 3-masted steamer was the world's largest ship; it served as a troopship in the Crimean War.

Iolanthe: torpedoed 10 miles off Portland Bill. 4.1.1918.

Jessie: sunk by submarine gunfire 7 miles off the Bill. 27.4.1917.

Kingston Cairngorm: naval trawler, mined off Portland Bill. 17.10.1940.

Kyarra: 4,500 ton steamer, torpedoed off Durlston Head. 26.5.1918.

Lord Stamp: 448 ton naval trawler, mined in Lyme Bay. 14.10.1940.

The Macbain: steamship, torpedoed 20 miles s.s.w. of Portland Bill. 4.3.1917.

Marguerite: French steamship, torpedoed off Lyme Regis. 28.6.1917.

Martha: steamship, torpedoed off Portland Bill. 7.3.1918.

Meknes: French liner, torpedoed off Portland. 19.7.1940.

Memnon: 3,203 ton steamer, torpedoed 20 miles south-west of Portland Bill with the loss of 6 lives. 12.3.1917.

Mermaid: sunk by bombs 18 miles s.s.w. of Anvil Point. 29.4.1917.

Motor Torpedo Boats' *90* and *92:* destroyed by fire in Portland Harbour. 16.7.1941.

Moidart: torpedoed with the loss of 15 lives 7 miles south-east of Lyme. 9.6.1918. A rare 20 cwt gun has since been salvaged from the wreck.

Orne: French steamship, torpedoed off Portland Bill. 21.12.1917.

Perriton: sunk by submarine gunfire in Lyme Bay. 29.1.1918.

Polkerris: French steamship, torpedoed off Portland. 4.3.1918.

Pomeranian: torpedoed 9 miles off Portland Bill with the loss of 55 lives. 14.4.1918.

Radaas: Danish steamer, torpedoed in Lyme Bay. 21.9.1917.

Recoil: naval trawler, mined in Lyme Bay. 28.9.1940.

Remindo: naval trawler, lost off Portland, cause unknown. 2.2.1918.

Romsdalen: torpedoed off Portland Bill. 17.2.1917.

Salsette: 5,842 ton steamer, torpedoed 15 miles south of the Bill with the loss of 15 lives. 20.7.1917. The *Salsette* had once been the fastest steamer in the P & O fleet.

Samson: The 32 gun *Samson* was one of an unknown number of ships that sank during the Battle of Portland, February 18th – 20th, 1653: the captain and most of the crew went down with their ship. The Battle was waged against the Dutch, and began when the 80 strong English fleet under Blake and Monck intercepted a Dutch convoy of 200 merchantmen and about 70 warships under Van Tromp. At least 30 Dutch merchantmen and 4 warships were sunk during the engagement, which began 3 miles off Portland and ended near the Isle of Wight.

Silverdial: tug, sunk by aircraft fire in Portland Harbour. 4.7.1940.

Sona: 519 ton yacht, destroyed by aircraft. 4.1.1942.

St Dunstan: dredger, mined off Abbotsbury with the loss of 2 lives. 23.9.1917.

Start: Norwegian steamship, torpedoed off St Alban's Head. 22.12.1917.

Tandil: 2,897 ton steamer, torpedoed 20 miles off Portland Bill with the loss of 4 lives. 12.3.1917.

Trito: steamship, bombed in Lyme Bay. 20.9.1940.

U.B.19: German submarine, sunk by Q-ship *Penshurst* off Portland Bill. 30.11.1916.

U.B.62: German submarine, sunk off Portland. 14.10.1917.

U.B.74: German submarine, sunk by depth charges from the armed yacht *Lorna* in Lyme Bay. 26.5.1918.

Valdes: 2,233 ton steamer, torpedoed 7 miles off Portland with the loss of 6 lives. 17.2.1917.

Warrior II: 1,124 ton yacht built in 1904 sunk by aircraft off Portland. 11.7.1940.

W.H.L.: steam vessel, torpedoed 8 miles s.s.e. of Portland Bill. 28.1.1918.

Bibliography & Acknowledgements

Boddy, Maureen. 'Dorset shipwrecks', a three-part article in issues 48, 49, 50 of *Dorset, the county magazine*.

Cozens, David. *Deep End, The Story of the Lyme Regis Lifeboats*, 1969.

Farr, Grahame. *Wreck and Rescue on the Dorset Coast, The Story of the Dorset Lifeboats*, 1971.

Hancox, David. *A Hundred Years of Life-Saving, 1869 – 1969: A History of the Weymouth Lifeboat Station*, 1969.

Hocking, C. *A Dictionary of Disasters at Sea, in the Age of Steam, 1824 – 1962*, 1969.

Laird, Clowes, W. *The Royal Navy, A History* Vol II, 1603 – 1714, 1898.

Matthews, Arthur. *A Descriptive and Historical Account of West Bay*, 1901.

Matthews, Harry C. *One Hundred Years of Life-saving at Sea: the story of the lifeboat service at Poole*, 1865 – 1965, 1965.

Millward, E.L. *Rescue, the Story of the Swanage Lifeboats from 1875*, 1953.

Payne, Donald. *Dorset Harbours*, 1953.

Zanelli, Leo. *Shipwrecks Round Britain, a Diver's Guide*, 1970.

British Vessels Lost at Sea 1914 – 1918, H.M.S.O., 1919.

Royal and Merchant Navy Losses, World War II, H.M.S.O., 1947.

A History of the County of Dorset, Volume II, V.C.H., 1908.

The following are the best accounts of individual wrecks:

'A Gentleman'. *An Authentic Account of the Hope, A Very Rich Dutch Merchant-Ship laden with goods and money, that was cast away on Portland Beach in the County of Dorset*, 1749.

Meriton, Henry & Rogers, John. *A Circumstantial Narrative of the Loss of the Halsewell (East Indiaman), Captain Richard Pierce*, 1786.

Pocock's *Authentic Narrative of the Loss of the Abergavenny, East Indiaman, off Portland*, 1805.

Smith, Charlotte. *Narrative of the loss of the Catherine, Venus and Piedmont Transports, and the Thomas, Golden Grove, & Aeolus, Merchant Ships, near Weymouth, on Wednesday the 18th of December last*, 1796.

Contemporary newspapers have provided much of the information about wrecks from 1820 onwards, as have issues of the *Life-Boat*, the *Annual Reports* of the R.N.L.I., Lloyd's Register of Shipping, the *Dorset Year Book*, and the *Annual Returns of Wrecks and Casualties*.

By happy accident, Miss Maureen Boddy's name appears first in the Bibliography. My debt to her is immense. Not only has she answered my innumerable questions, but she also most generously made available the files containing her extensive and pioneering work on shipwrecks in Dorset. I am also grateful to the Reading Room staff of the National Maritime Museum, Miss Margaret Holmes of the Dorset County Records Office, and Glanville J. Davies for allowing me to make use of his as yet unpublished paper, *Wreck and Plunder in Eighteenth Century Portland*.

I would also like to record my gratitude to the following for allowing me to make use of illustrations in their possession: The British Museum, Dorset County Library, Dorset County Museum, The Lyme Regis Museum, The Portland Museum, The Royal National Lifeboat Institution, The Weymouth Museum.